THE DAILY LECTIONARY

A weekly guide for
daily Bible reading
The Sundays after Pentecost
Year Two, Book Two

Joseph P. Russell

The Daily Lectionary

A weekly guide for daily Bible reading
The Sundays after Pentecost
Year Two, Book Two

A method of daily Bible reading that will add to our appreciation of scripture, and to our experience of worship and daily Christian living is provided by the Episcopal Church's The Book of Common Prayer, the Anglican Church of Canada's The Book of Alternative Services and The Lutheran Book of Worship.

In each of these we find a daily lectionary, a listing of passages of scripture for daily reading. The lectionary covers a two year cycle. After following the full cycle, the reader will have been exposed to all of the books of the New Testament twice and all of the pertinent portions of the Old Testament books once—pertinent because the daily lectionary does not include those portions of the Hebrew scripture that are redundant or irrelevant for the Christian. The Book of Psalms is read in its entirety every seven weeks.

The biblical texts follow the ebb and flow of the liturgical church year. Occasionally they reflect the Sunday texts assigned in the eucharistic lectionary. Since the liturgical seasons take us through the fullness of Christian doctrine, we are exposed week in and week out to all aspects of what it means to be alive in Christ. Of all the many methods of Bible reading, this one is tied most closely to what is going on in the rest of the church.

This pattern of Bible reading goes back to our Jewish roots where portions of scripture were (and still are) assigned for study each week. The entire assembly focused on the same texts. Though the texts were often read in the privacy of one's home, they were still read in communion with the rest of the assembly. This is the principle of the daily lectionary as it exists today in the Christian tradition. Some people will read the lectionary with a group of other worshipers. Others will read the scripture alone. But either way, they will read the Bible with the church. We are in communion with each other.

This weekly guide is designed to be read on Sunday or Monday. Just as you may find help in appreciating a film, concert or sporting event by reading program notes before the event, so you may find help in appreciating your Bible study by reading the program notes offered in this book. Comments provide an overview of the Old Testament, epistle and gospel texts assigned for the week. They include some background on the theological and historical setting along with the rationale for reading the texts during the particular season. Comments also give insight about the rites, hymns, customs of the church or our calling to act for Christ in the word. *Forward Day by Day* offers notes about the readings. Both resources are offered by Forward Movement to support you in your desire to understand and to be empowered by daily Bible reading.

A few notes for your consideration:

Forward Movement's *Daily Prayer and Bible Study with the Book of Common Prayer* will help you understand the structure of Morning and Evening Prayer, the context for the Bible texts assigned in the lectionary.

The daily lectionary readings are shown on pages 936-964 of The Book of Common Prayer; pages 452-475, The Anglican Church of Canada's The Book of Alternative Services; pages 97-99, The Lutheran Book of Worship.

The daily lectionary follows a sequential pattern of reading scripture each day beginning Monday and running through Saturday. With the exception of the Old Testament, the Sunday readings assigned in the daily lectionary usually have no connection whatsoever with the rest of the week. Therefore, only the readings appointed from the Old Testament for Sundays are considered.

The psalms are read on a seven-week cycle. The New English Bible with the Aprocrypha, Oxford Study Edition (also available in The Revised Standard Version) gives excellent, brief explanations of the psalms. You may want to read the psalms from the annotated Bible rather than from your prayer book on occasion so that you can appreciate the finer points. (See the psalm exposition and chart in volume 3.)

This volume includes notes for the season after Pentecost. In The Book of Common Prayer and The Book of Alternative Services the weeks are given numbered propers which are keyed to the calendar dates of the Sundays. These proper numbers do not correspond to the numbered Sundays-after-Pentecost shown on church bulletins and liturgical calendars. Look instead at the date assigned for each set of propers shown in the prayer book daily lectionary. To make following the daily lectionary easier, the Church Hymnal Corporation has published the texts for the lectionary in four volumes, avoiding the need to look up three different readings in the Bible each day. (*Daily Office Readings,* compiled and edited by Terrence L. Wilson, The Church Hymnal Corporation, 800 Second Avenue, New York, NY 10017.)

May scripture come alive for you as you become immersed in the world of the Bible with daily reading. May your life be empowered as you see more clearly the presence and power of God revealed through the pages of scripture. "For whatever was written in former days was written for our instruction, that by steadfastness and by the encouragement of the scriptures we might have hope" (Romans 15:4). We study the Bible not simply for an understanding of the past but for a clearer perception of how God is working in history and in creation today. This is what makes Bible study so exciting and so important for each Christian.

Blessed Lord, who caused all holy Scriptures to be written for our learning: Grant us so to hear them, read, mark, learn and inwardly digest them, that we may embrace and ever hold fast the blessed hope of everlasting life, which you have given us in our Savior Jesus Christ; who lives and reigns with you and the Holy Spirit, one God for ever and ever.

(The Book of Common Prayer, page 236)

Joseph P. Russell

3

Week of the Sunday closest to May 11

The Old Testament readings:

Ezekiel, the prophet, wrote during a traumatic time. Jerusalem fell to the Babylonians in 587 B.C. and Judah's leading families were sent off into exile in Babylonia. Ezekiel was one of the earlier exiles. Imagine the anguish of the exiles and the impression it made on them. Ever since the Israelites encountered the Lord at Mt. Sinai they had been warned by Moses and by the prophets that to turn away from the covenant would result in disaster. Now disaster was visited upon them.

Ezekiel wrote in visionary language, reflecting either ecstatic revelatory experiences or a literary style that helped the reader reflect on the mystery of God's action in that awful time. The book receives a very cursory treatment in the daily lectionary. We read from Ezekiel only in the seventh week of Easter in year one, and in this week.

Ezekiel used the metaphor of the watchman to describe the role of the prophet. One called by God has no choice but to speak the Lord's word, unless he would be responsible for the sins of those he failed to confront. The Lord wants repentance and not destruction. These words of mercy and comfort end our reading Monday. Our biblical ancestors felt they had an inalienable right to the land given to their ancestors. Not so, Ezekiel reminds them in Tuesday's reading. How can the people expect to possess the land when they have failed to keep covenant with the Lord? It is not theirs by right, but by the privilege of living within the covenant.

The image of Jesus as the Good Shepherd may come to your mind on Wednesday, for Ezekiel castigates the shepherds of Israel (the kings and leaders of the fallen nation) for not having watched over the people. Ezekiel's words are strong reminders of God's demand for justice and compassion to the neediest citizens of any nation:

> The weak you have not strengthened, the sick you have not healed, the crippled you have not bound up, the

strayed you have not brought back, the lost you have not sought, and with force and harshness you have ruled them (Ezek 34:4).

These words are important for government leaders in our time to keep in mind.

From the words of confrontation, during the last part of our week in Ezekiel we focus on beautiful words of hope and promise: ". . .they shall be my people, and I will be their God" (Ezek 37:23). Though Israel had fallen because of her wickedness, the nation would be restored so that all nations could know the holiness of the Lord. This is a statement that expresses the role of the church in today's world. The church reveals God's grace and holiness so that the world may know the Lord as shepherd.

Our week in Ezekiel closes with the image of the living waters flowing out from under the restored Temple in Jerusalem. The living water of God will enrich and cleanse all of creation. Jesus used the metaphor to describe the work of the Holy Spirit that would come after him (See John 7: 37-39).

The second readings:
We'll be reading the First Epistle of John the next two weeks. It is a late New Testament writing, coming from the same hand, or at least the same school of writing, as the Gospel of John. The author of the epistle saw the church tempted to compromise the gospel in the face of growing resistance and heretical teaching. The epistle calls the church back to the gospel as it had originally been received, and it reminds the church in strong words that to follow Christ is to love and serve Christ's people in the world.

Monday's reading has the feel of the first 18 verses of the Gospel of John. You may want to read those opening words to appreciate the place that 1 John has in the New Testament. On Tuesday you will read familiar words, part of the comfortable words after the confession in Rite I of the Holy Eucharist:

". . .if any one does sin, we have an advocate with the Father, Jesus Christ the righteous; and he is the expiation for our sins, and not for ours only but also for the sins of the whole world" (1 John 2:1-2).

The ethical implications of this epistle as it reflects the meaning of the gospel are made clear in Tuesday's reading: "He who says he is in the light and hates his brother is in the darkness still" (1 John 2:9). We cannot claim a personal relationship with the risen Christ and hate our neighbor and brother. (Jesus' words from the Sermon on the Mount expand this commandment: "But I say to you, love your enemies and pray for those who persecute you. . ." (Matt 5:44a).

Those baptized into the Body of Christ at Easter were anointed with oil as a part of the baptismal ritual. Christians are not to forget their anointing and what it meant, we are reminded in Thursday's reading: ". . .as his anointing teaches you about everything, and is true, and is no lie, just as it has been taught you, abide in him" (1 John 2:27b).

Our reading from 1 John ends the week with a strong reminder of the ethical imperative inherent in the gospel. What has been handed on to us is the command to love as Christ loved—an active, vital, self-giving love. If we see someone in need and do not respond, then God's love cannot be in us for all the talk of being Spirit-filled.

The Gospel readings:
Monday's and Tuesday's readings from the Gospel of Matthew provide us with summaries of all that Jesus did that showed his power to save, even to the point of bringing life to the dead. These are proclamation stories told to convince the unconverted and to strengthen the faith of the church. As we move into chapter 10 on Tuesday, we begin reading the second major teaching section of the gospel. The 12 disciples are named, and for the balance of the week we read Jesus' instructions to them. As Matthew put together sayings of Jesus into a Sermon on the Mount, he also collected sayings appropriate

to the training of the disciples. The Gospel of Matthew was written partly as a manual of instruction to the early church.

Jesus saw his personal ministry as being limited to the Jews. His first instruction to the disciples about going only to the lost sheep of Israel, read on Wednesday, was countered in his final commissioning to the disciples at the time of the resurrection. (See Matthew 28:19).

Travel light and don't waste time with people who are not open to the coming reign of God. Don't let possessions and problems keep you from proclaiming the reign of God in word and act. These are instructions for Jesus' disciples and the primitive church.

Persecution is guaranteed for the disciples, Jesus warned. The reign of God comes into inevitable conflict with the standards of the present age, and people will resist. Jesus' words about the coming of the Son of Man, read on Thursday, may seem confusing as we look back through nearly 2,000 years. Jesus warned his followers to live with the constant expectation that the end of the age and the Lord's day of judgment were imminent.

In 70 A.D. Jerusalem and the Temple were destroyed. For Jesus' people this was, indeed, *a* day of judgment if not *the* day. In our own time we can see events that point to final judgment, crisis times when we stand under judgment as a person, as a nation and as a society.

Saturday's words are harsh. Jesus did not come to bring peace, but the sword. That is the experience of the church, of Christian martyrs, prophets and activists throughout history. Think of the Christians in Germany who opposed the Third Reich, the Martin Luther Kings, men and women who stood for the gospel against oppression and injustices, Christians persecuted in Central America. There can be no compromise with evil, even when it means standing against one's family.

Week of the Sunday closest to May 18

The Old Testament readings:

Most of the writings of the Old Testament seek the wisdom implicit in the *story* of God's relationship with his people as a *people*. It is the wisdom of the story told by the historian, the teller of legends, the prophet, and by the priest as he recalls the story in ritualistic acts. But after returning from exile, the Jews came to appreciate a type of writing popular in other nations around them—wisdom literature. This kind of writing does not deal with the *story* and its interpretation, and it does not focus on the community of God's *people*. Rather it uses *non-narrative* forms and seeks for truth as it applies to the *individual* who wishes to live a happy life.

The Book of Proverbs comes out of this postexilic time. Paging through it, the reader can quickly see that it is filled with short proverbs not unlike the "Confucius say" style familiar to the joke teller. But underneath these proverbial sayings is the unique Jewish understanding that the heart of all wisdom is awe and worship ("fear") of the Lord. To seek after wisdom is to seek after the Lord.*

The readings for the next two weeks are portions of the Book of Proverbs. In the opening chapter, not assigned for reading, Proverbs is attributed to King Solomon's reign, but his name was used because of his reputation for great wisdom.

On Monday, Friday, and Saturday wisdom is given a feminine personification. "She is more precious than jewels, and nothing you desire can compare with her" (Prov 3:15). In chapter 8 you will read that wisdom was created by God at creation and has been with God ever since. Wisdom was seen as a direct gift from God. To seek wisdom was to seek God. Wisdom was no mere body of knowledge, but that aspect of God that seeks

---

*(Joseph P. Russell, *Sharing Our Biblical Story* Minneapolis, Minn.: Winston Press, 1979; pp. 60-61).

to inspire men and women with the awareness of God's will for them. Since the dawn of creation "she" has been seeking to communicate God's wisdom to man and woman: "The Lord created me at the beginning of his work, the first of his acts of old" (Prov 8:22). Compare that statement with the powerful poem that provides an overture for the Gospel of John: "In the beginning was the Word, and the Word was with God, and the Word was God..." (John 1:11). If you replace "wisdom" for "word" in John's prologue you get a sense of how Christ was understood by John and the primitive church.

That aspect of God that reaches out to man and woman took on flesh in Jesus. Wisdom became incarnate, enfleshed, in the man Jesus. Wisdom became a man personally reaching out to people to bring them the nearer knowledge of God. "Jesus is the wisdom of God," Paul declared in 1 Corinthians 2:24.

There can be no more important goal in life than the acquiring of wisdom, we are reminded on Tuesday. Turn to 1 Kings 3:4-15 and read Solomon's prayer for wisdom. The Lord came to the king in a dream and promised a rich reward for Solomon, who sought wisdom above power and prestige for himself.

Much of our reading this week is framed as wise sayings of father to son. Loose women form a major section of this fatherly advice. On the surface, the Book of Proverbs may not seem the most illustrative reading assigned in the daily lectionary, but if you consider the theological implications of God reaching out to humanity to reveal the creator's presence and will, these simple sayings may take on added meaning for you.

The second readings:
We continue reading 1 John. Keeping the commandments of Christ is the only way of truly being his follower. We are to believe in the gospel given to the church. Jesus is the Christ, the Son of God, and we must love in the way that he showed us in his life, suffering and death. Whoever keeps these commandments "...abide in him, and he in them..." (1 John 3:24a).

These words are paraphrased in the prayer of consecration:". . .that he may dwell in us, and we in him" (BCP, p. 336).

Monday's reading sets forth a standard of faith, belief that "Jesus the Christ has come in the flesh." This orthodox statement would set the true follower of Christ apart from those coming into the church with heretical doctrines that denied that Christ was both man and Son of God.

On Tuesday we read a summary of the gospel: "God is love, and he who abides in love abides in God, and God abides in him" (1 John 4:16). These words are soon followed by the warning: "If anyone says, 'I love God,' and hates his brother, he is a liar; for he who does not love his brother whom he has seen, cannot love God whom he has not seen" (1 John 4:20).

Wednesday our reading opens with a simple statement of faith that circulated in the early church: "Jesus is the Christ." This creed must be on the lips of the Christian just as acts of love must shape the life of the Christian.

Christ is synonymous with life, we learn on Wednesday, for he came to overcome the world through his baptism (the water) and his death (the blood). The letter ends with strong words of forgiveness for the sinner. Notice how similar the closing words of this epistle are to the closing statements of the Gospel of John. Compare 1 John 5:13 with John 20:30-31.

Friday's and Saturday's readings come from the two very short epistles of 2 John and 3 John, probably also written by the writer of 1 John. These are brief personal notes, sent with the same concern as 1 John. The church, the "Lady" in 2 John, must hold fast to the doctrine she was first taught. Third John deals with strife within the church presided over by the writer's friend, Gaius.

The Gospel readings:

On Monday we conclude the section on teaching the disciples and begin a new one, dealing with increasing controversy with the Jews, along with a series of Jesus' parables. Words about John the Baptist open this section. The least of those who have accepted Jesus are greater than John because they have personally experienced the breaking in of the reign of God. John was only the announcer of this day.

Strong words of condemnation spoken by Jesus are heard this week. He is beginning to run into the blindness and disbelief of his own people. The feelings of frustration and anger are evident. Even the people of Sodom would have responded more than the people of towns Jesus has been visiting!

In the Jews' attempt to discover Wisdom by intricate study and practice of the Torah, they have made themselves blind to the possibility of the new covenant in their very midst. "You can't see the trees for the forest," Jesus might have said. Jesus' yoke is lighter than the yoke of the Torah that the Jews took on so willingly. The simple and uneducated could respond to Jesus. They are far humbler because they know their righteousness can never be earned by study or ritual practice.

Sabbath practices are the issue in Friday's reading. In the strict keeping of the Torah nothing that even vaguely resembles work can be done. And yet, Jesus quickly points out, the Temple priests themselves "work" in the act of carrying out their duties. King David, when he first escaped from King Saul, used sacred bread to survive (1 Samuel 21:1-9). Surely Sabbath and ritual laws should not be followed to the point where they take precedence over compassion and healing.

Saturday's reading may not be clear. Jesus quotes from Isaiah's suffering servant songs, describing one who is to come whose suffering for justice will bring redemption and healing to all the people. The suffering servant referred to in the poems could have been a collective reference to the role of the Jewish people in history, but Christians quickly identified Jesus as that suffering servant and Jesus makes that identification himself in this text.

Week of the Sunday closest to May 25

The Old Testament readings:

We'll conclude our reading of the Book of Proverbs this week, so don't let the long series of wisdom sayings exhaust you. They provide us with some insights about the values Jesus' ancestors held. Remember that he would have been raised on these ancient sayings. Some would have framed his imagery as he spoke with people. For example, Sunday's reading uses the metaphor of a great banquet held by Dame Wisdom in which she offers the fine wine of wisdom. Think about a parable Jesus told: "And again Jesus spoke to them in parables, saying, 'The kingdom of heaven may be compared to a king who gave a marriage feast for his son, and sent his servants to call those who were invited...'" (Matt 22:1-3). The imagery of a feast becomes the setting of a parable told by Jesus to speak of the kingdom of heaven.

For the most part you will be reading a series of proverbs this week. You may feel as if you are opening a stack of Chinese fortune cookies by the time Saturday comes! The sayings are not so random as they may appear, however. They were grouped by the final editors of the book.

The second readings:

We spend this week in the First Letter of Paul to Timothy, one of the three "pastoral epistles," so called because each deals with the pastoral concerns of the primitive church. Scholars disagree about whether these epistles were written by disciples of Paul at a later date or are, indeed, from the hand of Paul himself, written at the time of his imprisonment in Ephesus or Rome.

The familiar saying, "Christ Jesus came into the world to save sinners" (1 Timothy 1:15), is seen in its biblical context on Monday. The writer was obviously quoting a saying in circulation within the church. It could have been a creedal statement or a fragment of a hymn. Tuesday's reading, 1 Timothy 1:18—2:8, includes directives for the church at prayer that still guide us as we share the prayers of the people at the Holy Eucharist. On Wednesday, qualifications for bishops (the Greek word is *episkopos)* and deacons are given in 1 Timothy 3:1-16. Significantly, only two orders of ordained ministers are listed here.

In 1 Timothy 5:19, assigned for Friday, we come across the Greek word, *presbyteros,* translated "elder." John Calvin and John Wesley saw this as evidence that bishops and elders were really one order of ordained ministry, rather than two. They based this claim partly on the scripture read this week. It was on this authority that Wesley, ordained in the Church of England as a *presbyteros,* reasoned that he had the authority to ordain others.

Watch for another ancient Christian hymn in 1 Timothy 3:16: "He was manifested in the flesh, vindicated in the spirit. . ." We can say that the first hymnal of the church was the New Testament itself—enriched by a tradition of hymns and canticles, and with texts from the Old Testament.

"For the love of money is the root of all evil. . ." (1 Timothy 6:10). Sound familiar? The writer of this epistle may have picked up a saying familiar in the ancient world and used it to illustrate his point.

The Gospel readings:

The reference in Monday's reading from Matthew about the unforgivable sin of slander against the Holy Spirit may come as a surprising statement in the light of Jesus' many words of forgiveness and grace. One way of interpreting Jesus' enigmatic statement is to realize that if a person attributes the gifts of the Holy Spirit to the devil or fails to recognize the gifts at all, then that person cannot be open to the possibility of God's forgiveness in this age or in the age to come.

Jesus' frustrations with his own generation are felt again on Tuesday. The Queen of Sheba (or Queen from the South) had sense enough to journey to Jerusalem to hear the wisdom of God's chosen king, Solomon. The people of Nineveh had wisdom enough to repent and thus escape destruction. They didn't waste time asking Jonah for a sign. They acted when they heard his word of warning. The present generation is so wicked and blind that they demand a sign before they will believe.

We are in the midst of a section of Matthew's gospel devoted to the controversies Jesus had with the Jewish authorities and with the disbelief of the people with whom he came in contact. If Jesus' words sound harsh, realize the struggle he was undergoing. Let us not picture him a dispassionate Son of God with no human feelings and responses. He deeply feels rejection and conflict, but more importantly, he sees his own people turn away from the gift of participating in the reign of God that he has come to announce. Wednesday's words about unclean spirits returning to an empty house are a picturesque way of saying, "you've got to replace the evil with something good. You have to replace hate with love, injustice with justice, or your last situation will be worse than the first." Jesus' words about his family may seem particularly harsh, but the true family of Christ are those who respond to the urgency of the new age.

The parable of the weeds, read on Thursday, may have been altered by the church. A concern in the writer's time was that there were people in the church who were not living out the gospel. An allegorical explanation of the parable is read Saturday, expanding the focus to include judgment of all people at the end of time. Friday's parables—the mustard seed and the leaven—remind us that God's kingdom may seem imperceptible at the present moment, but it will grow to unbelievable size.

Week of the Sunday closest to June 1

The Old Testament readings:

Most Old Testament writings assume one can discover the mind and purpose of God. Moreover, the good and righteous person who lives in harmony with God's purpose, will live a life filled with blessings. The wicked person may appear to be prospering today, but in the end will get the punishment deserved.

The Book of Job raised serious questions about those assumptions. The Book of Ecclesiastes goes even further in questioning how much one can know of God and how much satisfaction one can expect to gain in this life. The book comes close to ridiculing Israel's whole idea. What makes the book meaningful as we read it these next two weeks is that the questions the writer raised are the questions every person raises. If you are accustomed to quick comfort in biblical and devotional readings, you will be in for a surprise. There is no happy ending to Ecclesiastes, at least not in the original writing. A final editor did manage to put a few positive thoughts on the scroll to make it a little more acceptable to orthodox positions of Judaism.

Incidentally, the strange name of the book is from the Greek word that means "one who speaks before an assembly" or "who is a member of the assembly." The word, ecclesiastical, meaning something that pertains to the church, comes from the same Greek root. The church is the people assembled. As you read, you may wonder how the book was accepted into the Old Testament. Notice in the very first verse that the writer claims to be ". . . son of David, king in Jerusalem," in other words, Solomon. Though the book may have been written as late as 250 BC, the ascription to Solomon helped the book gain acceptance. Perhaps the nature of the writer's questions, common to everyone, may also have contributed to its acceptance into the Old Testament.

The theme is clearly stated in Sunday's reading: all of life is vanity or emptiness. Would having everything in life that one wanted bring ultimate happiness? The author wrote in the name of Solomon, who had everything. Was Solomon really satisfied? asked the author. No, he was not. It was all emptiness in the end, we read on Monday.

Wednesday's reading contains words popularized in contemporary song and literature" "For everything there is a season, and a time for every matter under heaven..." (Eccles 3:1) and the times just keep revolving, so what's the point of life? "God has made it so, in order that men should fear before him" (Eccles 3:14). All one can do is stand in awe of God and creation.

By Friday you may be in need of prayer, but the writer of Ecclesiastes warns you to keep your prayers simple and think about the words you use. Don't make a fool of yourself!

Wealth will not bring satisfaction, we discover on Saturday. The income tax was not part of the writer's experience, but he knew well the feeling of wealth bringing worry. One wrong decision can dissipate wealth amassed over a long period, leaving the next generation nothing. We end the week as we began. All of our efforts are nothing but vanity and emptiness.

The second readings:

Paul traveled through the province of Galatia on his first and second missionary journeys, a territory now part of Turkey, north of the island of Cypress. He preached a gospel that was free of the restrictions of Old Testament law. Circumcision of males was not necessary, nor the intricate dietary laws. None of those ritual practices could bring salvation. The only thing that would bring new life was faith in the risen Christ. Life in Christ was a free gift, an act of grace that could not be earned, only appreciated.

This was the hope-filled message Paul had taken to Galatia, to the cities of Derbe, Iconium, and Lystra. Read chapter 14 of Acts for details of Paul's adventures in that province. Gentiles and some Jews were converted to the gospel. They were baptized into the new life of the body of Christ. Paul rejoiced with these converts. He formed them into churches, trained leaders, established the teachings of the gospel, healed the people, and then departed from Galatia with the confidence that his work would be carried on faithfully.

Now it is about 54 A.D., and Paul may be in the city of Ephesus. Much to his utter frustration, he has heard that the people of Galatia have accepted a different gospel than Paul's. A "circumcision party" has arrived on the scene, claiming that Paul's gospel of freedom from the strictures of Jewish law was not correct. To be a Christian, one must also be a Jew. Circumcision and all the other facets of the law must become a Christian's burden as well as a Jew's. As if the teaching were not bad enough, the people were buying it! Paul's teaching and work was going down the drain. His authority was being undermined. This letter is not quite as angry as 2 Corinthians, which we read a few weeks ago, but a stiff one, nevertheless. We feel Paul's hurt and frustration, along with his determination to re-establish his authority as an apostle who brought the true gospel.

Paul wastes no time getting into the argument, we discover on Monday. He moves right in to establish his authority, independent of the apostles in Jerusalem. His experience of the resurrection on the road to Damascus has an authority of its own, he points out. If he was to speak with conviction on freedom from the Law, he must show his credentials, and those credentials must not be seen as secondary, else his teaching would be compromised.

In the text assigned for Tuesday, Paul writes about an agreement with the apostles in Jerusalem. They would honor his missionary work among the gentiles, while Cephas (another name for Peter) would concentrate on Jewish converts. The gentile Christians were not to be forced to accept the Jewish ritual law that included circumcision and strict dietary practices. Jewish Christians were to accept gentile Christians as brothers and sisters in Christ. Cephas obviously went back on the agreement, we discover on Wednesday, for Cephas refused to associate with gentiles on a visit to Antioch. Paul writes with bitterness about his confrontation with Cephas and other Jewish Christians.

If we think the primitive church lived in peace and tranquility, our eyes are quickly opened with this chapter from Galatians. Obviously, Peter and Paul had strong words right in front of the people.

Galatians 2:17-18, assigned for Wednesday, is a little hazy. Paul's point is that if we are to believe that the Christians' reliance on Jesus alone for salvation, rather than on the codes of Torah, was a cause of their falling into sin, then it would follow that Jesus had caused them to sin. Absurd! And if Paul were to go back to accepting the Law as a way of salvation, then he would be acknowledging that he has been teaching the wrong thing to gentiles. Also absurd.

The New English Bible translation for Galatians 3:1 begins: "You stupid Galatians. . ." Can you picture the people of Galatia reading this letter for the first time? Paul is angry, and he leaves no doubt about that anger. The point he is making in this chapter is that Abraham was justified, or made righteous, by God because he had faith. Only later did the covenant, or Law, made with Moses on Mt. Sinai come along, but that did not cancel out the original agreement. Paul is using arguments from the legal system here. The Law was really just a "baby-sitter," or temporary measure, until the time came when the true descendants of Abraham could live once more in faith. It was the sinfulness of those earlier descendants that forced God to lay down the Law, so that the people could see more clearly their transgressions. But since no one could keep the Law perfectly, no one could be made righteous through their vain attempts to follow it.

As a matter of fact, Paul goes on to explain, the Law really levels a curse against everyone who attempts to follow it, since in the Book of Deuteronomy it clearly states that those who do not "abide by all things written in the book of the law. . ." will be cursed (Gal 3:10). Jesus deliberately entered into the curse of the Law when he allowed himself to be "hanged on a tree." Deuteronomy specified that a man put to death for a crime was to be hanged on a tree until sunset as a sign that he was cursed (Deut 21:22-23). Jesus, who was hanged on the cross, or tree, was the righteous Son of God, proof positive that the Law was impotent or meaningless. The mere hanging on the tree did not make the blessed one cursed. That's proof that the Law bears no weight in the new covenant made through Christ. Paul's legal mind is not always easy to follow, especially when we are not so familiar with the Torah.

Saturday's reading closes our week with the beautiful words: "There is neither Jew nor Greek, there is neither male nor female; for you are all one in Christ Jesus (Gal 3:28)". We are all children of God, a relationship that transcends the empty legalism of Law and ritual.

The Gospel readings:

Monday's reading emphasizes the need to reorient one's life toward the kingdom of God. In the parables of the treasure found in the field and the merchant finding a fine pearl, the lucky persons sell everything to enjoy the new-found treasure, and so it must be with us as we respond to the gospel. The closing words are rather subtle. The scribe or teacher who knows and loves the Torah and has discovered the reign of heaven has the distinct advantage of both the old and the new teaching. Such a statement would fit well with a Jewish Christian audience!

With Wednesday's reading we begin a new section of Matthew. Jesus prepares the disciples to lead the church. We'll be in this major teaching section for the next two weeks, through the end of chapter 17. The death of John the Baptist colors our reading on this day with a grim and foreboding feeling. John died in witnessing for God in the face of evil.

The story of the feeding of the 5,000 comes Thursday. It can be seen as a foretaste of the messianic banquet, just as the Eucharist is a foretaste of our life to come at God's table.

On Friday we read of Jesus' walking on the water. He is about to pass the disciples by when he notices their fear. Jesus exercises power over the elements by calming the storm. The waters represented death and chaos to ancient peoples. Some scholars feel that this may have been a resurrection appearance. The power of the story in the early church lay in the hope that the event held out to Christians living in confusion, persecution and fear.

Think about Paul's controversy with the Jewish authorities as you read Saturday's lessons. Paul's authority for insisting that gentiles could enter into relationship with Christ without following the strict dietary rituals of the orthodox Jew comes from these passages. Holiness has not to do with what goes into us, but what comes out of our lives. We dare not substitute empty ritual for life-giving service to the Lord. Realize the radical nature of these words as you read them. The ancient practices followed by generations of faithful Jews is questioned. Can we understand the reaction of the Jewish authorities to Jesus' words and actions? How do we respond in church and nation to those who question the very heart of our actions and assumptions about life?

Week of the Sunday closest to June 8

The Old Testament readings:

Jesus may well have had the portion of Ecclesiastes assigned for Sunday in mind when he told the parable of the rich fool (Luke 12:13-21). "God gives wealth, possessions, and honor, so that he lacks nothing of all that he desires, yet God does not give him power to enjoy them, but a stranger enjoys them..." (Eccles 6:2). The influence of the Old Testament on the mind of Jesus is evident as we become familiar with Hebrew scripture.

Monday's reading may sound strange at first hearing, for it seems to say that death and mourning are better than birth and feasting. The sense of this text is that one is better off having proved oneself than to be starting from scratch as an infant. One is better off being seriously aware of life and the possibility of suffering and death than innocently carrying on with laughter like a fool with no thought of ultimate consequences.

"Eat, drink, and be merry for that is about all you can be sure of in life," is the gist of Tuesday's reading. The theme for the whole book is picked up again in the opening lines of the reading: "This is an evil in all that is done under the sun, that one fate comes to all..." (Eccles 9:3). Wisdom really doesn't amount to much anyway, since when the wise person could add insight, no one listens or remembers. That point is made Wednesday with a brief story about a city under siege, where the people ignored the possibility of learning from the wise man. The reading of Ecclesiastes ends Friday with an allegory describing the growing darkness of old age and impending death. Final editors have attempted to lighten the message of Ecclesiastes with a few verses at the end of the book. God will set things right in the end, is the hopeful theme of the addition.

Saturday begins an historic trek through Numbers, Joshua, and Judges that will go on until the middle of August. We pick up the great history of Israel that was interrupted in the daily reading as we approached the feast of Pentecost. Rejoin our biblical ancestors on their pilgrimage from Egyptian oppression to liberation with Moses. At Mt. Sinai they are receiving instructions from God, mediated through Moses. Much of what we study in this section reflects customs and practices that Israel established generations later when they settled in the land of the Canaanites.

We meet the Levites, a tribe set apart to perform duties in the Temple. Their special role among the tribes symbolized the relationship all Israel had with the Lord. According to Exodus 34:19-20, first-born males in every family were to be dedicated, or sacrificed, to God, a common custom among ancient peoples. The Levites' dedication to God was a substitute for those first born in other tribes.

The second readings:

Paul's denunciation of those who would lead the Christian Galatians into following the ritual practices of Judaism continues to ring in our ears this week. Circumcision was anathema to Paul, for it meant Christians had no faith in the grace of Christ, but must earn salvation through empty rituals. Paul's message of grace was being undercut by the "Judaizers." How could the young Christians possibly fall for their line when they had followed Paul's gospel of freedom with such enthusiasm only a short time before!

More personal details about Paul are hinted at in Monday's reading. Apparently he was sick when he first arrived in Galatia. It was his sickness that gave him an opportunity to preach and minister to the people. Paul used a story from the Book of Genesis to form an allegory of life under the "gospel" of the Judaizers and life under the gospel he preached. Abraham's first son was born to his slave, Hagar, who was later driven out into the wilderness. Hagar represented the covenant made with Moses at Mt. Sinai (the old testament or covenant). The son born to Sarah was the son of promise, Isaac. The new covenant, or testament, people are related to that great patriarch.

Paul's anger led to some strong statements. Wednesday's reading closes with the admonition, "I wish those who unsettle you would mutilate themselves!" (Gal 5:12 RSV). *The New English*

Bible is clear: ". . . make eunuchs of themselves!" as is the *Jerusalem Bible:* "I would like to see the knife slip!" Paul did not mince words!

Beginning with Galatians 5:13, we move into a section about what life under the freedom of the gospel is to be like. "What are we going to do as a result of our freedom?" is the focal point. Paul even directed the Galatians to pay their teacher. Paul pointed to the authenticity of his letter, closing it with his own hand, using "large letters." Paul often dictated his letters to a scribe. We can picture his taking up the pen as he concluded this letter of frustration.

The Gospel readings:
Notice Jesus' exhaustion as you begin Monday's reading. Jesus would retreat for awhile, but rest is impossible. A gentile woman demands a healing. Jesus' blunt words to her may shock us: "It is not fair to take the children's bread and throw it to the dogs" (Matt 15:26) but the tone of his voice and the expression on his face are not seen or heard by us. In any case, the woman throws his words back to him. Perhaps amused at her quickness, he responds to her request. Ironically, it is a woman considered by some "unfit to receive the children's bread" who shows the faith in Jesus that "the children" themselves lack. Perhaps it is the irony of this situation that causes Jesus to speak to the woman so bluntly, using an expression of disdain applied to gentiles in Jesus' time.

Last week we read that Jesus fed 5,000 people, and now we read that Jesus fed 4,000 people. Many scholars feel that this is a doublet, or repeating of one story.

Wednesday's reading contrasts being blind and having true sight. The Pharisees demand a sign from Jesus who denies that God would send signs "in this generation." The disciples, however, have been seeing signs all around them as they follow Jesus, especially in the miracle of the loaves! Despite the signs, they remain blind to their significance.

Yeast, or leaven, was a common metaphor. Evil rises up in life, infecting all of society, just as yeast rises up in dough.

(Yeast, a metaphor for evil, is removed from Jewish households at the time of Passover to this day.)

The writer of Matthew provides scriptural authority for Peter's key leadership role in the church. If you compare Matthew 16:13-20 with Mark 8:27-33, you will see that the latter text lacks the words of commissioning to Peter. Matthew's concern was to provide stability for the young church as it moved from direct experience with the risen Christ into an institutional form. Peter is to be the "rock" upon which Jesus would build his church. This is the scriptural authority for the church to act for Christ from one generation to the next. What the church decides on earth is ratified by God. The church acts, in other words, with the authority of God. This passage may explain the primary position given to the Gospel of Matthew in the New Testament.

The Episcopal, Roman Catholic and Orthodox churches, moreover, see this passage as establishing the authority of leadership exercised by the bishops of the church. The apostolic authority of Peter has been handed down with the laying on of hands from one generation of bishops to the next. The bishop of the church points directly to the authority to "bind and to loose" granted to Peter.

The name Peter means "rock." Jesus was making a pun as he gave Simon the added name of Peter. The Rock soon earned himself the dreaded name of Satan because he could not accept the idea that Jesus must suffer and that his followers must suffer as well. Jesus' temptation to follow evil did not end in the wilderness; it came from his closest disciple. Jesus' calling each disciple to take up the cross may contradict expectations we have been raised with, too. These words of Jesus confront our values and visions of life just as they did Peter's.

Jesus' promise that the Son of Man would come before the present generation passed away can be seen either as an unfulfilled expectation of Jesus or as one that was at least in part fulfilled with the resurrection and the coming of the Holy Spirit to the disciples.

On Saturday you may want to look back to Exodus 24:1-18 in order to appreciate the significance of the transfiguration.

Moses went "up into a cloud" to receive the Law. Jesus takes Peter, James and John with him "up into the mountain" for a revelation of the new Law, which is Jesus, a law not written on stone, but written on the hearts of the people. (See Jeremiah 31:31).

Several other points need to be kept in mind: Elijah was the great prophet of Israel who lived in the time of King Ahab and Queen Jezebel (1 Kings). Tradition held that Elijah would return at the coming of the Messiah to herald the day of the Lord. The Feast of Booths was a joyous fall harvest festival in which shelters were erected from harvest stalks and vines to celebrate God's presence with the people as they wandered in the wilderness. According to Zechariah 14:16-19 all nations would celebrate that feast together at the day of the Lord. Peter's mention of the tent (or booth, or tabernacle) is a reference to that great expectation. Elijah's role, ushering in the day of the Lord, was to purify the people, to turn them back to Torah. Jesus saw this tradition fulfilled by John the Baptist. Jesus was not to be confused with Elijah. He was to be the suffering servant of the Lord, who would die so that healing and salvation might come for all people.

Week of the Sunday closest to June 15

The Old Testament readings:

The origins of our liturgical prayers, rituals, and traditions are imbedded in scripture. A blessing frequently heard in public worship opens this week's reading in the Book of Numbers: "The Lord bless you and keep you..." (Num 7:22). Israel was led out of Egypt by a pillar of cloud by day and a pillar of fire by night. (The paschal candle carried in the darkness of the Easter vigil liturgy is a symbol of that pillar of fire, who is for us Christ, leading us to salvation and liberation.)

The cloud continued to lead the Israelites through the wilderness, we learn on Monday. It settled over the Tent of Meeting, or Tabernacle, a movable tent-like structure that served as a temple, where Moses went to pray and where the Ark of the Covenant was kept during encampments. This cloud indicated where the people were to move and how long they were to stay in a place. The story that the pillar of cloud led the people is contradicted by an account of Moses begging his father-in-law to stay with him because he could point out the way to go through the wilderness.

Notice in Numbers 10:35-36 an ancient liturgical formula used by priests when the Ark was moved in battle.

We first hear of the manna of the wilderness in Exodus 16:9-26. Manna, though poetically described as "bread from heaven," was probably a natural phenomenon still found in the Sinai today. "The manna was probably that sweet and sticky substance excreted by insects sucking the sap from tamarisk bushes. This kind of edible material is still found in the central valleys of the Sinai, especially in June and July. The Arabs spread it on bread."*

The constant bickering and complaining of the Israelites led poor old Moses to despair. (When reading of Moses and the Israelites, I picture a station wagon load of children on a long,

---

Jerome Biblical Commentary (Prentice Hall, 1968) p. 90

27

tiring trip crying out for food, or rest, or the answer to the in-evitable question, "When are we going to get there?")

The Lord responded to Moses' cry for help: ". . . I will take some of the spirit which is upon you and put it on them. . ." (Num 11:17). Those are the words Moses heard the Lord say to him in a moment of inspiration. Leadership must be shared. "Send them forth in the power of that Spirit to perform the service you set before them. . ." the bishop prays at the time of laying on of hands in the liturgy of baptism/confirmation.

> Therefore Father, through Jesus Christ your son, give your Holy Spirit to N (name); fill him (her) with grace and pow-er, and make him (her) a priest in your Church.

These are words the bishop prays at the time of the ordina-tion of a priest. (BCP, pp 309, 533) The roots of these two pray-ers go back to our forefather, Moses, in the wilderness when some of the Spirit which was upon him was bestowed on seventy others so that they might share leadership in the Lord's name.

The quail dropping at the feet of the Israelites is also a natural phenomenon still found in the Sinai. Migrating birds fly over the desert and become exhausted. Our people, however, in-terpreted all acts as signs of God's favor or displeasure. We, too, are called to thank God for what others may consider sim-ply acts of nature. The Lord feeds us the natural foods that sus-tain us, and we are called to respond by offering our lives in faith.

Spies sent into the Promised Land returned to report that there were quantities of produce but also huge people that struck fear into the hearts of the scouts. Only Joshua and Caleb wanted to invade the land. The Lord's punishment for lack of faith was quick to come. This generation would not see the Promised Land. They were doomed to continue wandering the wilderness. Their children would inhabit the land. The peo-ple looked frantically for leaders who would take them back to Egypt. Slavery was better than following the strange God of Moses. Lest we condemn our biblical ancestors too harshly, we must reflect on our own lives. The safe harbor of the known is often preferred to the unknown risk of movement, even when the present situation is filled with pain and "enslavement."

It was Moses' intercession before God that saved the people from immediate destruction. Moses was the constant mediator between an unfaithful people and the liberating Lord who called the people out of slavery. Moses' case before God was practical: Destroy the people in the wilderness and the rest of the nations will talk!

"The Lord is slow to anger, and abounding in steadfast love, forgiving iniquity and transgression. . ." (Num 14:18). These are the descriptive words of the Lord's mercy that close our week of reading in the Book of Numbers.

The second readings:

Paul's Epistle to the Romans will be our subject for the next six weeks. This is the greatest of Paul's letters, the most complete statement of what he understood to be the gospel of Jesus Christ. All of Paul's other letters were written to particular people about particular problems. They knew Paul personally. They had heard him preach and knew his theological stance, so when he wrote to them he simply filled in the cracks—clarified statements he had made while with them.

The Epistle to the Romans, on the other hand, was Paul's "primer in the Christian faith" to a group of Christians whom he longed to visit, but had never met. He wrote an extended letter of introduction, giving his credentials, laying out his understanding of the gospel, and making a place for himself in their midst when he could finally visit them. Paul did not know he would finally meet these people as a prisoner of the Roman government! Scholars don't know where Paul was when he wrote this letter, but some feel he wrote Galatians shortly before Romans. With Galatians fresh in our minds, look for Paul's development in Romans of ideas he began to explore in the earlier letter.

After Paul's greeting, he moved quickly into stating his major thesis:

For I am not ashamed of the Gospel. It is the saving power of God for everyone who has faith—the Jew first, but the Greek also— because here is revealed God's way of righting wrong, a way that starts from faith and ends in faith, as scripture says, "He shall gain life who is justified through faith" *(New English Bible,* Rom 1:16-17).

Paul next explains the need for that saving power of God. Everyone, Jew and gentile alike, have turned to wickedness, and all stand in judgment before the Lord. Though the gentiles do not live under the Law of the covenant, they have a natural law. They should be able to see God in the natural order of life and respond to love and creativeness with faith and right actions. Instead, people turn to self-worship and immoral practices. But the Jews, who felt that they were righteous because they were circumcised and followed the ritual acts of the covenant, were condemned even more severely than the gentiles, for the Law made even clearer how far they had turned from God in sin.

The Law, in other words, condemns rather than saves. "For it is not the hearers of the Law who are righteous before God, but the doers of the Law who will be justified"(Rom 2:13). "For he is not a real Jew who is one outwardly, nor is true circumcision something external and physical. He is a Jew who is one inwardly. . ." (Rom 2:28-29). No wonder Paul was so furious at the Judaizers who came to the province of Galatia to insist on circumcision and the outward allegiance to the covenant. But, Paul pointed out, Christians must always remember that it was the Jews who were entrusted with the wisdom, or oracles, of God in the first place. It was the Jews who revealed God's word and presence, even in their unfaithfulness. God will be faithful to the covenant made with the Jews even if they are unfaithful.

A familiar question raised in response to Paul's preaching occurred to him as he continued to write his letter: "If a person's sin helps to point up God's justice, should that person be condemned?" "If my wickedness and lying serve to make God look better, why should God be angry with me?" was the concern raised by Paul's audiences. Paul dealt with this question later (chapters 6 and 8). Here he only acknowledged the problem some were having with his teaching.

The week in Romans ends on a somber note. All stand condemned, Jew as well as gentile. The Law that the Jew relied on for salvation only condemned the Jew by pointing up the sinfulness of each person.

The Gospel readings:

We ended our reading last week with the mountain top experience of Peter, James and John in the scene of the transfiguration, a scene reminiscent of Moses' encounter with God on Mt. Sinai. When Moses came down from the mountain, he was met with confusion and loss of faith on the part of the people (Exodus 32). They had created a golden calf to worship. As Jesus comes down from the mountain he also meets with the loss of faith, and confusion among his disciples. No wonder his anguished words: "How long must I put up with this people?"

Tuesday's reading includes a strange dialogue between Jesus and Peter about paying the Temple tax. Jesus tells Peter that paying the tax is appropriate for the disciples though, as his followers, they are exempt from the obligation. They can pay it out of courtesy, so as not to offend the Temple authorities. Jesus directs Peter to look for the coin with which to pay the tax in the mouth of a fish. He might have said, "Go ahead and pay the tax out of respect and to avoid scandal. God provides you with the means of payment with the fish you catch every day."

On Wednesday we move into another of Matthew's teaching sections, this one directed to the primitive church. Matthew placed principles of communal life laid down by the church side-by-side with Jesus' sayings remembered by the church, providing a basic guide for church authority and administration.

To enter into the reign of God, we read on Wednesday, one must adopt the attitude and nature of a child. This refers to the child-like sense of innocence, but it also requires that we live as children under the authority of God.

Thursday's reading lays down clear guidelines for the church in settling disputes among the faithful. Last Thursday in Matthew 16:13-20 we read that Peter could act for heaven in binding up and loosing. This Thursday we notice that the church is given that same authority. Wherever two or three make decisions, it shall be "done for them by my Father in heaven" (Matt 18:19). "For where two or three are gathered in my name, there am I in the midst of them (v. 20). Here we see the early church's realization that Christ was calling them to gather to seek his guidance and to act in his name. These are very early statements of church policy that still govern our life in the church today.

Guidelines for the primitive church continue on Saturday with Jesus' words about divorce. If Torah allowed divorce, Jesus insists, it was only because God knew that the people were hard of heart and could not live up to God's intentions. Not so for the Christian. God created male and female to live as one. What God has joined together must not be separated. The celibate life is held out as an alternative to marriage, a unique statement found only in Matthew and in Paul's writing.

Jesus' words seem restrictive in our age when divorce is recognized by the church. Remember that in Jesus' day wives could be easily divorced by their husbands and had very few rights of their own. Jesus' teaching on divorce protects the woman and affirms her status in her husband's house. Historically, the church has exercised the privilege of modifying Jesus' teaching in the light of the guidance of the Holy Spirit. Matthew 18:18 is an example of the way the church, since earliest times, has interpreted and modified Jesus' teachings to fit new situations. In Mark's account of Jesus' words on divorce (Mark 10:10-12), there are no exceptions. Matthew, writing a few years later and to a different audience, adds "except for unchastity," allowing one exception.

Week of the Sunday closest to June 22

The Old Testament readings:

"No faith, no Promised Land," was the grim reality that greeted our biblical ancestors, we learn as the week begins. The entire adult generation who left Egypt with Moses would leave their bones in the wilderness. Their children would enjoy the promise lost to a faithless generation. In desperation the people tried to do for themselves what they did not have faith in the Lord to do for them. They tried to invade the land of the Canaanites and failed miserably.

Two revolts against the authority of Moses arose simultaneously. Korah's revolt had to do with the right to serve as priests. "For all the congregation are holy, every one of them, and the Lord is among them; why then do you exalt yourselves above the assembly of the Lord?" was Korah's complaint (Num 16:3). He was stating a concern for generations to come. The priesthood of all believers was a rallying cry of the protestant reformers of the 16th century. Why should there be some set apart to mediate between the people and the Lord, when the Lord calls all people out to be servants and ministers?

Control over leadership was the issue in the revolt of Dathan and Abiram. Moses and Aaron had done a terrible job of leading the people, the argument went. They had not kept their promises. It was time to replace them with true leaders, and Dathan and Abiram would be glad to fill the bill. It sounds as if we are in the midst of a political campaign!

The Lord answered the theological and political points of contention very directly. Dathan, Abiram, and their families were swallowed up, along with Korah and his followers. Two hundred and fifty men holding incense were burned in a mighty fire from the Lord. These stories were told around campfires and family meals for generations before being written down. Realize that the narrative was heightened in the process of telling and retelling the stories.

Behind the stories lie historic incidents, but if God had shown the kind of direct miraculous power described in these chapters, then it is difficult to imagine further rebellion against the authority claimed by Moses.

Midway through Wednesday's reading we again find the Israelites complaining and testing Moses' authority to lead them. How much impetus for rebellion would be left if the earth had opened up to swallow rebellion and fire had come from heaven? Theological reflection is always woven in with historical narrative so that what we read in scripture is both the root of a historic incident along with a theological reflection that often takes the form of highly exaggerated details. "This is what the death of those men in the camp last night meant," the contemporary interpreter would say. "God opened up the earth and swallowed rebellion alive," the biblical writer explains.

The budding of Aaron's staff is another theological reflection that assures the generations of readers that the only true Temple priesthood was Aaron and his descendants. Aaron's death comes at the end of the week's reading. His son, Eleazar, would carry his priesthood into the Promised Land at last.

Again, Moses' leadership was tested. The people were thirsty. Why did Moses bring them out into this desolate, God-forsaken place to die, they asked. The Lord spoke into the mind of Moses again, this time announcing a further sign of blessing: water would appear from a rock. Moses took the opportunity sarcastically to chastise the people for their constant demands. Rather than standing back with word of prayer alone as a means of producing water from the rock, he showed his own strength by striking the rock with his staff. The Lord's condemnation was quick to come. This is one interpretation of God's sudden anger at Moses in Friday's reading.

The second readings:

Justification by faith is the theme of the section of Romans that greets us as our week opens. Faith is often used today as a body of doctrine: "What is your religious faith?" "I'm an Episcopalian," may be my response. But faith, for Paul, was an action word. "From what I've heard of this surgeon, I will trust my life to her and undergo the necessary surgery," is what Paul meant by faith. I can jog, I can diet, I can pay my physician's bills on time, but the true test of whether I'm really open to be healed (salved, saved) by that physician is whether I can put my life on the table. Faith results in action, in a changed life, in a total trust in the Lord's power. Nothing can make us righteous before God but our faith.

Another turning point in Paul's teaching is that none of us can possibly earn God's grace. The parable of the prodigal son (Luke 15:11-32) comes to mind. The younger son was accepted by the father even before the words begging for acceptance were out of his mouth. Nothing he could have done would have earned his sonship back with his father. The gift of life as a favored son was offered freely.

The sacrificial language of the New Testament does not always strike a responsive chord for the contemporary reader because Temple sacrifice is not a part of our life as it was in Paul's time. If one sinned in biblical times, then one had to pay for that sin with a sacrifice to God—an animal, a bird, or a grain offering. The pure lamb offered at the Passover in the Temple "died for" the sins of the family offering the lamb. Its blood was a sign of covenant and forgiveness. Christ was the final sacrifice, made for the sins of everyone ever to be born, Paul stated. The idea of a God who would not demand some kind of payment was alien to Paul's way of thinking. A just God would have to receive payment.

Paul responds to the unseen questioner again as Monday's reading closes. Faith does not undermine the Law, so sacred to Israel. Rather, the Law, given for the righteousness of God's people, has now been truly realized in the gospel of Jesus Christ.

I'd suggest taking a few minutes before reading Tuesday's and Wednesday's texts to look back at the stories of Abraham and Sarah in Genesis 12:1-9, 15:1-21, 17:1-27, and 18:1-15. The faith shown by Abraham became a model of the faith we are to have, and Abraham showed that faith generations before there was a Law!

God's unbelievable grace that leads to human liberation and

freedom from the enslavement to sin becomes the focal point for the balance of the week. In the healing love of Jesus Christ came the realization that God's love is far more powerful than human sin or any evil that comes into the world. Adam is the symbol for the sinful nature of every man and woman. Christ is the living experience of God's forgiving grace.

Well, if our sinfulness serves to point up God's goodness, shall we not sin all the more? Of course not, responds an indignant Paul. When we were baptized, we entered into Christ's death. We died to our old, sinful ways. And when we were baptized, we entered into the new, resurrected life of the risen Christ. How can one talk of going back to what we are dead to? The words spoken by priest or bishop at the time of baptism reflect Paul's theology of baptism: "We thank you, Father, for the water of Baptism. In it we are buried with Christ in his death. By it we share in his resurrection. Through it we are reborn by the Holy Spirit" (BCP, p. 306).

The Gospel readings:

Jesus' words read on Monday say it is impossible for the rich and powerful to enter the kingdom of God. We may try to modify those words and set them aside in our affluent culture, but Jesus saw clearly that it was the poor and powerless who responded to his words, his healings, and his presence. These people knew their dependence on God. The church, during the time the written gospels were developed, experienced the same phenomenon. It was the poor and the oppressed who responded to the gospel. The writer of Acts recorded that converts sold all their possessions and shared what they had as each person had need. There is a complete reversal of life when God's reign comes. The "first shall be last" and the last shall be first" is a common theme throughout the New Testament.

On Wednesday we read the parable of the laborers in the vineyard. Those hired last receive the same pay as those hired at the earliest hour of the day. God's gracious love is offered completely to all who accept the invitation to "labor in the vineyard." There can be no privilege that comes with seniority.

Discipleship also results in a reversal of expectations, we learn Thursday. James and John expect reward and prestige; instead they will receive the cup and baptism of martyrdom. One who is a disciple is one who serves, rather than one who is served. Think of the impact of those words on a church suffering from persecution. Think of the impact of the words on the church in Central America, South Africa and other places where Christians suffer for their faith and their convictions.

Each day in our reading we move closer to Jerusalem. Friday's walk with Christ brings us to Jericho, twelve hard, uphill hours from the great city. Through faith, two blind men, whom Jesus meets outside Jericho, receive their sight. They can see and their response is immediately to follow Jesus. The invitation is to leave *our* blindness to the gospel behind and to follow Jesus ourselves, even if it means Jerusalem and the cross.

Saturday we stand with the crowds who greet jesus on his triumphal entry into Jerusalem. In order to appreciate this traditional Palm Sunday passage, you need to keep a few facts in mind: The horse was a beast of war and conquest, while the ass was a sign of peace. When a king came on an ass, it meant he came to announce a reign of peace and justice. The spreading of garments and branches on the ground was an ancient sign of greeting to the king. (See 2 Kings 9:13 for an Old Testament example of this custom.) At the Jewish feast of Tabernacles (also called the Feast of Booths) and again at Hannukah, branches were waved and words from Psalm 118:25-26 were shouted by the people. Hannukah celebrated the rededication of the Temple when the Greeks were driven out in 164 B.C. The Feast of Booths was celebrated as an annual renewal of the covenant between God and the nation. It was also a time of recalling the years of wilderness pilgrimage in which God led them toward the Promised land. One of the images of the coming reign of God was that all nations would keep the covenant and join the Jews in Jerusalem for the great Feast of Tabernacles. (See Zechariah 14:16-21.)

"Hosannah" meant "save now!" in Hebrew. As we reflect on the ancient traditions associated with Jesus' entry into Jerusalem, we can see both the political and religious impact of his action. In a sense, Jesus was acting out a living parable of his life and death.

Week of the Sunday closest to June 29

The Old Testament readings:
More of the same! Poor Moses found himself dealing with an unfamiliar, bickering, complaining people as he led them through the wilderness of Sinai. As a result, he found himself having to act as mediator between them and the Lord who had called the people forth from Egyptian slavery. When the Israelites' camp was infested with poisonous serpents, the people saw the event as God punishing them for their lack of faith. When Moses prayed to the Lord to forgive the people, the Lord guided him to make a bronze serpent that could be held up high for all the people to see. Those who looked at the bronze serpent would be saved. The writer of the Gospel of John used this event as a metaphor to describe Jesus' role as savior to the world: "And as Moses lifted up the serpent in the wilderness, so must the Son of man be lifted up, that whoever believes in him may have eternal life" (John 3:14). As you read these stories, realize that the events have been given theological interpretation over years of sharing. As Israel reflected on the experience of an infestation of poisonous snakes, they came to understand the event as divine punishment. Moses, as intercessor, would have heard the Lord's word in his thoughts and prayers and would have acted accordingly.

Last week's reading described how Israel backed away from the king of Edom when he refused permission to pass through his kingdom. Moses found an alternative way to move into the land of the Canaanites, avoiding direct confrontation with Edom. This week we find the Israelites engaging in victorious battle against the Amorites, who also denied them passage. Encouraged by their victory, the Israelites moved north to do battle with Bashan; again they won a major victory. From that battle they moved south to a point opposite Jericho. Having now gained a reputation for winning fierce battles, the approach of the nomadic horde of Israelites causes Balak, king of Moab, to cringe in terror. The delightful story of King Balak's attempt

39

to get Balaam to curse Israel occupies our attention from Monday until Saturday.

We do not know much about Balaam. He was considered a powerful enough dispenser of blessings and curses to warrant being summoned by a king. His spells must have worked before. Though he spoke reverently of Israel's God, there is no indication that he was related to the Israelites. The story of Balak and Balaam consists of two or three once separate accounts that were finally woven into one narrative. The poetic portions of the assigned chapters are the most ancient pieces of the story. The weaving of at least two accounts into one narrative becomes evident on Tuesday. Monday's lection ends with God giving permission to Balaam to follow Balak's emissaries and see the king. But Tuesday's lection opens with Balaam, riding his faithful ass, traveling along. The Lord is described as being angry because Balaam was going to see King Balak, a direct contradiction to what we have just read. The Lord's anger came to Balaam in the form of a fiery angel blocking the road. At first only the donkey can see the angel.

What we are to remember in this account is that nothing can obstruct the will of the all-powerful God of Israel. The story becomes a theological statement. "God's will be done," says the Lord's Prayer, and God's will is indeed done in this story.

Picture a nomadic people sharing this tale around the campfire. There would have been laughter at the appropriate places. A balladeer may have offered the poetic portions in song, to the accompaniment of a stringed instrument. Hear the laughter of our biblical ancestors as they listen to the story of poor Balak becoming more and more agitated as the expected curses against Israel become blessings instead. There was no stopping Balaam. We leave him cursing all of Israel's future enemies, as well as the present adversaries.

The second readings:

"For the wages of sin is death, but the free gift of God is eternal life in Christ Jesus our Lord" (Rom 6:23). These words set the theme for our week in Romans. To the complaint raised that Paul's teaching would lead people to sin all the more, since their sinfulness would serve as proof of God's mercy, Paul responded that once grace is accepted a person is under a new master. Sin is no longer the power in one's life, for God's empowering Spirit is in command. How, then, could one want to go on sinning?

Paul stated in Tuesday's reading, that the Law was defeating and not life-giving, convicting one of sin by making the sin clearer, but not helping the person defeat sin. When I see the 35 mile per hour speed limit sign, it convicts me of my sin as I glance at my speedometer and find I'm doing 55. The blue flashing lights in the rear view mirror announce that judgment is near, but the sign has not saved me from the sin. Moreover, the Law awakens the sinful desire within me. As Paul reflected on the Law of the Torah and the attempts to make himself righteous, he finally threw up his hands in despair. The harder he tried to do what was right, the more he stood hopelessly convicted of his sinfulness. It was as if there was an unseen power within him placing him in alienation with his own being as well as with God. What was he to do? That question heads us into the next section of Romans.

Freed from sin, we're filled with the Holy Spirit. We're not left at the mercy of sinful impulse. We're not free to sin so that grace may abound. We have a new destiny in the Spirit, and the Spirit dwelling within us makes us sons and daughters of God. We can actually address the awesome God as "Abba," or "Daddy." Now nothing can separate us from the love of God. The suffering we experience is our participation in Christ's suffering, a suffering that leads to the redemption of the world. Here is an area of theology we saw Paul developing in his letter to the Galatians. As Paul shared his struggles with the people of Galatia, he shared with them the conviction that his suffering was a way in which he could participate in Christ's on-going act of salvation for the world. Pain and struggle took on a healing, empowering quality for him. Paul drew on his personal experience to make generalizations about the redeeming quality of suffering that all Christians share. The struggles of the present would give way to the birth of the new age. Present pain was like the birth pains of a woman in childbirth. All creation cried out, anxiously awaiting the birth that was coming. What a remarkable statement!

Incidentally, Romans 8:14-19, along with additional verses from chapter 8, are appointed in The Book of Common Prayer for reading at a burial. These words provide a sense of hope at the moment of death.

Though Paul talked as if sin were already defeated, he also pointed forward to the time when this victory would finally be realized. There is a "here, but not yet" quality to what Paul wrote in Romans. Sin is defeated, and we have a new master in the Holy Spirit. We can call God our parent and be free from the urging of sin, but we are really living in expectant hope of that vision becoming a reality: "For in this hope we are saved. Now hope that is seen is not hope. For who hopes for what he sees? But if we hope for what we do not see, we wait for it with patience" (Rom 8:24-25).

The Gospel readings:

A little background is necessary to appreciate the cleansing of the Temple scene. Jesus was not upset with the money changing and selling going on in the Temple. That was essential. It was unfair practices that aroused his anger. But more important, Jesus was acting out a prophetic drama to announce the inauguration of the messianic age. Take a moment and read Jeremiah 7:1-16, Isaiah 56:7 and Malachi 3:3-5 so you can see Jesus' activity in the same perspective as the people of his time. You may also want to read Jeremiah 13:1-11 and Isaiah 20:1-6 for examples of similar dramatic actions by the prophets.

The curse of the fig tree, read on Monday, can best be understood as a parable told by Jesus (see Luke 13:6-9) that the writer of Matthew (and Mark) placed in the narrative to emphasize the point of what was happening in these final days.

Jesus' actions at the Temple were not lost on the authorities. They moved quickly to entrap him in order to discredit him among the people and to find grounds on which he could be brought before the Jewish and Roman courts.

The parable of the vineyard read on Wednesday would have aroused the anger of the religious authorities instantly. Those who do not care for the vineyard will be cast out and others will be given rights as tenants. Read Isaiah 5:1-7 to see the inspiration for this parable.

The parable of the wedding feast read on Thursday confronts the institutional church of our own day. We, like the Jews of Jesus' time, are invited to be God's witnesses in the world, but it is often the outcasts whom God must bring in to sit at table. We are bound by our possessions and worldly responsibilities, too busy and involved to respond. Verses 11-14 seem to introduce a separate parable about a man who came to a wedding banquet without the proper dress. The point of this second parable differs from the first. Here the man is condemned because he had not prepared for the event. He, like the young maidens who did not purchase enough oil for the night watch, is thrown out into the night. (See Matthew 25:1-13.)

Friday's reference to paying taxes to Caesar is not meant to imply that there are two separated realms of responsibility in the world, the sacred and the secular. The "things that are God's" are everything in heaven and earth, if we take the Torah seriously. It is lawful to pay taxes to Caesar so long as Caesar does not contradict the ways of God.

Jesus' controversy with the religious authorities of his day becomes more intense as we read from the Gospel of Matthew on Saturday. Though the Pharisees believed in the resurrection, the Sadducees refused to accept the doctrine. Thus is it the Sadducees who seek to discredit Jesus on the subject of the resurrection by raising an impossible problem arising out of the Law regarding a brother's responsibility to marry the wife of his deceased brother. Jesus' response moves the argument beyond life as we understand it today to life as God wills it for us in the age to come where marriage customs have no meaning. Jesus quotes from Exodus 4:15 to make the point that God spoke to Moses about the ancestors of the Jews as a living people: "Say this to the people of Israel, 'The Lord, the God of your fathers, the God of Abraham, the God of Isaac, and the God of Jacob, has sent me to you.'"

Week of the Sunday closest to July 6

The Old Testament readings:

As Moses' death drew closer, he had to live with the reality that he was not to enter the Promised Land because he had displeased the Lord in the wilderness of Zin. (See my remarks on page 28.) Instead, Joshua would receive some of Moses' authority and lead Israel into the land of the Canaanites. That word "some" is important. Where Moses had direct inspiration from the Lord, Joshua had to rely on Aaron's son, Eleazar, who would consult the Urim for guidance. Scholars have no record of exactly what the Urim was. It was probably a form of lots that were cast by the priest, providing a "yes" or "no" response to specific questions. Notice that Moses lay hands on Joshua as a sign of the authority from God that was passed on from one to another. Here we see the origins of the laying on of hands at confirmation and ordination. The sacraments and rituals of the church have ancient roots.

The details for providing cities for the Levites and cities of refuge for persons who had killed accidentally are set forth in Tuesday's lection. Again, we come across the origins of present practices. Churches in the past and in our day sometimes provide sanctuary for refugees and persons sought by the authorities. The Torah provided for such sanctuary so that an accidental killer could not be harmed by the injured family seeking revenge. When the high priest dies, such killers would be pardoned and allowed to return home with their safety assured. The Levites needed special provision for their living since they would be serving in the Temple and thus would not be able to earn income or purchase lands.

We move into the Book of Deuteronomy midweek. We'll be reading just a few selections from Deuteronomy to complete the narrative about Moses. Deuteronomy purports to be a sermon from Moses offered to the people just before he died. In this writing, Israel's struggle in the wilderness is remembered. The people were not to forget the painful lessons they learned in that generation of wandering. Every seventh year (the sabbatical year) at the feast of Tabernacles, Deuteronomy was to be read to the people as a way of remembering. Hearing the scroll read would lead them to repent of their sinfulness and return to the Lord. We, too, are called to read scripture so that we will remember the mighty acts of God in the past and align our lives more closely with the will of God revealed in scripture.

Friday's reading includes the first few lines of a song attributed to Moses. The heavens and the earth witness to the words spoken before the people, words that fall like refreshing rain on grass. Moses' death on Mt. Nebo, after looking into the Promised Land, marks the end of this week's selections.

The second readings:

The Holy Spirit leads the Christian to cry out "Abba, father," because the Spirit makes the Christian a son or daughter of God. In the same way, the Spirit groans within us so that we can communicate with God in ways that we cannot even comprehend. The Spirit is able to say for us what we do not have the power, courage, or insight to pray for ourselves.

A note of predestination is heard on Monday: "For those whom he foreknew he also predestined to be conformed to the image of his Son..." (Rom 8:29). The term, predestination, is often used erroneously to mean that God orders certain things to happen and certain people to be saved, while condemning others to damnation. Paul used this term simply to say that the Lord called out the church from among the peoples of the world to witness to the risen Christ and to share in the death and resurrection of Christ. Before Christ, Israel had been destined to witness to God's presence and power in the world.

Tuesday's text is often heard at funerals. It is one of the options suggested in the burial office of The Book of Common Prayer. Nothing, not even death, can separate us from the love of God!

Paul's deep love for the Jews caused him to turn his attention to their status under the gospel. Chapters 9 through 11 directly deal with this issue. First, Paul recalled the gifts God gave to Israel. He mentioned seven privileges, or gifts, given to Israel. The list concludes with the gift of the Messiah, or

Christ. But what happened to this promise, if it had now been taken from Israel and given to the Christians? Drawing from a brief survey of the patriarchs of Israel, whose stories are told in the Book of Genesis, Paul reminded his readers that God can freely choose which child to favor, even when the Lord's choice goes against natural selection. Thus Jacob, the second son of Isaac and Rebecca, was chosen over the first son, Esau. God can show mercy and love to whomever he chooses. Just as the Lord hardened the Pharaoh's heart in the time of Moses, so the Lord can harden the heart of the people at any time. Those who would question God must realize that the creature cannot possibly fathom the mind of the creator, any more than the pot can question the potter.

We can hear Paul's adversaries in the crowd raising questions as we begin Thursday's reading: "If God directs people in their actions, including 'hardening their hearts,' then how in the world can people be blamed for their sinful actions?" One cannot question God, Paul responded strongly. Be excited, rather, that the Lord is showing mercy and grace in the midst of life's struggles. Rejoice over God's mercy, rather than question God's justice. Paul spoke with sadness. His own people were so busy trying to earn their salvation by keeping the "jot and tittle" of the Law that they could not discern the grace of God through Christ and receive salvation as a gift. The very "stone" that could bring the Jews salvation instead becomes a stumbling block. Paul borrowed the metaphor of the stone from Psalm 118 and applied it to Jesus.

Friday's selection contains perhaps the earliest creed. "Jesus is Lord," was the simple statement of the Christians (Rom 10:9). By the middle of the second century that three-word creed had expanded into the Apostles' Creed, a statement of faith made by those who were giving themselves to Christ in baptism. The Nicene Creed was adopted by the church in the early years of the fourth century.

The Gospel readings:
From Monday through Wednesday we read strong words of

denunciation against the religious authorities of Jesus' day. To feel the power of these words, we need to apply them to the religious authorities of our own day. How does the church "...tithe mint and dill and cummin," while neglecting "the weightier matters of the law, justice and mercy and faith..." (Matt 23:23).

On Thursday we move into chapter 24, a section of the Gospel of Matthew that deals with Jesus' concerns about the end of the present age. The whole chapter is a collection of sayings and parables about the final times that will come before the new age is ushered in. If you want to impress your friends or Bible study companions, call this the "eschatological discourse." Eschatology is a technical term in theology meaning the last things of life, from the Greek word meaning last or extreme. These last times will be soon, Jesus warns. Struggle and persecution are seen by Jesus as a part of the final times. Though Jesus' words would have formed a basis of Matthew's writing, they also reflect the destruction of the Temple in Jerusalem that had just happened as Matthew wrote his gospel.

In 70 A.D. the Romans responded to a Jewish rebellion by destroying the Temple and the holy city. Jesus foresaw the destruction of Jerusalem that came after his death as a sign that the new age of God was dawning. Out of the ashes of the old, the new kingdom of God would be built. The Temple in Jerusalem would be replaced by the living temple that is Jesus' presence in the world. (The indwelling of the Holy Spirit will make each person a living temple of God, Saint Paul wrote. See 1 Corinthians 6:19.) Jesus used the language of apocalypticism to describe the dawn of the new age. Read Daniel 12:1-3 for a flavor of this style of literature that lies behind Jesus' words. The thrust of the message is that God is soon going to intervene to bring the present age of darkness to an end and usher in a new age of God. It is these days of final trial that some scholars feel Jesus may have been referring to when he taught us to pray, "save us from the time of trial." (The version of the Lord's Prayer you may be more familiar with inaccurately translates this phrase, "And lead us not into temptation.")

Week of the Sunday closest to July 13

The Old Testament readings:

We move out of the Book of Deuteronomy this week and begin the extended deuteronomic history that traces Israel's history from the conquest of Canaan in about 1220 B.C. to the time of the Babylonian exile in the year 587 B.C. This historic narrative is found in the books of Joshua, Judges, 1 and 2 Samuel, and 1 and 2 Kings. The history was probably written shortly before or during the time of King Josiah, who reigned in Judah from 640 to 609 B.C. However, the history continued to be written and edited right up to the time of the exile. The writers wove together the ancient oral stories of the people, told for generations.

Some stories had already been placed on scrolls by the time the deuteronomic writers started their work. They edited the written accounts and wove in additional narrative. Thus, you will find in your reading during the coming weeks places where the same incident is told from two or three different viewpoints. The deuteronomic writers and editors included as much of the tradition as possible in their works.

The result is more than a history; it is a continuing theological statement. The incidents as they are recorded help us understand how our biblical ancestors saw God working in the history of the peoples of the world and in the creation that provides the environment of history. There is a clear theological bias presented in the way the stories are told. When Israel followed the provisions of Torah, the nation prospered, battles were won, wealth was accumulated, and the people were satisfied. At any point where the nation was disobedient, however, immediate punishment from the Lord was felt. To suffer was to know that one had gone against the Lord's will.

This simplistic understanding of our relationship with God was later questioned by the prophets and wisdom writers of Israel and Judah, but the principle still influences our thinking to this day. "What did I do to deserve this," is a question that sees adversity as divine punishment. Events in Israel's history were perceived through the theological views of the deuteronomic writers. Nothing happened accidentally. All things pointed to God's blessing or to God's wrath. "Only be strong and very courageous, being careful to do according to all the law which Moses my servant commanded you; turn not from it to the right hand or to the left, that you may have good success wherever you go" (Joshua 1:7).

Seven verses into the Book of Joshua we read the theological purpose statement of the deuteronomic history. Israel was to follow the Lord's way so that Israel could prosper in the land the Lord had given her for an inheritance.

We meet Rahab the prostitute on Monday, the woman who hid Joshua's men as they moved into Jericho to spy in preparation for siege and conquest. Rahab quickly offered a creedal statement of fear. She and her people had heard all that the Lord had done for Israel, and they stood spiritless, waiting for the conquest. Her agreement to keep the spy mission a secret guaranteed safety for her whole family. The writer of the Gospel of Matthew included Rahab in the geneology of Jesus (Matt 1:5). Her faith makes her an important figure in Israel's memory.

The story of the crossing of the Jordan provides a means of raising up Joshua's authority, received from Moses in the laying on of hands at Mt. Nebo (Deut 34:9). As the Sea of Reeds dried up so that the Israelites could cross, so the river Jordan stopped flowing so that the Israelites, led by the Ark of the Covenant, could cross over on dry land. The stopping of Jordan's flow may have been a natural phenomenon caused by mudslide or earthquake, or it could have been already shallow from weeks of drought, but Israel saw it as the direct intervention of God acting on behalf of the people.

One reads the signs of history and nature as revelations from God. Israel took courage in the face of saving events. As this story was told over and over, the miraculous nature of the account would be heightened, much as we tend to heighten the impact of the stories we tell that have intense significance for us.

Memorial stones from the bottom of the Jordan were collected by each tribe so that the children of the coming generations would have cause to ask, "What do these stones mean?" Israel must remember; memorials, rituals, and traditions are still followed by Jew and Christian alike so that we may ask, "Why do we do these things?" The question leads to the telling of the story of God's mighty power in history and in creation.

The first celebration of the Passover marked a transition for the Israelites. No more would they be fed the "daily bread" of the wilderness. They would enjoy the fruits of the land at last. The Passover would serve as a "memorial stone" for all coming generations, for with the Passover every Jew must recount the experience of the Exodus. In the process of celebrating the Passover, each generation of children would ask the question, "Why is this night different from all other nights?"

Joshua encountered the "commander of the army of the Lord" in a vision that matched Moses' vision of the burning bush in the Sinai wilderness. In both instances, the instructions are the same: "Put off your shoes from your feet; for the place where you stand is holy" (Joshua 5:15).

The second readings:

In this week's reading of Romans, Paul revealed the mystery of God's plan of salvation. The hearts of the Jews were hardened by God so that they would not perceive the Christ and know the love and mercy of the Lord. But the salvation of the gentiles, in turn, would eventually cause the Jews to accept Christ. God's mercy would be revealed to them. No longer would the Jew look to Torah for a means of righteousness. Now they would know Christ as the true means of salvation, for Christ would open to them the possibility of divine grace.

Paul used quotations from the Old Testament to fortify his point. Elijah despaired that there were any faithful people left in Israel at the time he fled Jezebel's wrath and went into the wilderness. The Lord assured him that there was, indeed, a faithful remnant who would take up the witness of God. The church, the body of Christ, was the new remnant. But Christians had better be humble as they found themselves caught up in this divine plan. They were chosen by the grace of God and not for anything they had done. They were grafted onto the consecrated root that was Israel, a root that could not lose its favored calling by God despite the unfaithfulness of the people over countless generations. God still loved the Jews and when they were finally grafted back onto the root, that would be a great day for the ultimate glory of God.

"I appeal to you therefore, brethren, by the mercies of God, to present your bodies as a living sacrifice, holy and acceptable to God, which is your spiritual worship" (Rom 12:1). These words in Thursday's reading find their echo in the eucharistic prayer of the church: "And here we offer and present unto thee, O Lord, our selves, our souls and bodies, to be a reasonable, holy and living sacrifice unto thee" (BCP, p. 336). What we offer at the Eucharist is not money, service or an hour of devotion, but our entire lives as a living sacrifice, a sacrifice expressed in the symbols of what we have and who we are.

Saturday's reading urges Christians to obey civil authorities as they represent the authority of God. This passage has been used to justify the Christian's blind obedience to government. Paul wrote out of his life experiences. The Roman government had often protected him from the wrath of his own people. He wrote at a time when he could hope that the Christian church might somehow find legitimacy in the empire. He wrote as a citizen of that empire himself. Paul's words cannot be applied *carte blanche* to fit all situations and all governments. Throughout the history of the church, Christians have found themselves standing against the government as a direct witness to the higher authority of God. Scripture provides many examples of this great witness, examples that are not neutralized by Paul's words of advice to the church in Rome.

The Gospel readings:

Three powerful parables of coming judgment fall in rapid succession Monday, Tuesday and Wednesday. All of them speak to the same concern. We must be ready for the coming of Christ. We will be judged on our readiness. We must be ready at every moment. Paul echoed Jesus' words when he wrote to the

Christians in Rome: "Besides this you know what hour it is, how it is full time now for you to wake from sleep. For salvation is nearer to us now than when we first believed; the night is far gone, the day is at hand" (Rom 13:11-12).

The parable of the talents is not an encouragement for capitalism. We will not be judged by how much interest we've earned on our investments in this world. Rather it is about how we perceive our gifts and the God who grants them to us. How much are we willing to risk for the sake of the gospel? The servant who hides his talent has a perception of the master that would keep *anyone* from risking. "Master, I knew you to be a hard man..." (Matt 25:24). The first two servants were not limited by such a perception.

The parable of the last judgment is a vivid statement about our call to live with constant concern for others. To feed the stranger is to respond to Christ.

Wednesday's reading describes Jesus' anointing by a woman at Bethany. Jesus saw the woman's act as a fitting preparation for his burial, but we can also see a further symbolic act taking place. Israel and Judah's kings were anointed as a sign of their authority as kings. The Hebrew word for "anointed one" is translated "messiah;" in Greek the word is "christos." This woman, who is to be remembered for her act, may be seen as anointing Jesus as Messiah at the same time that she is anointing him for his burial. The cross points beyond death to Christ's victorious reign as God's eternal Messiah.

The Last Supper becomes our focus on Friday. You must keep in mind the traditions of the Jewish Passover to understand the implications of this meal with the disciples. As usual, Jesus takes the traditions of his people and forges new meaning out of the familiar. Lambs were slaughtered at the Passover as a sacrifice for the sins of the people. Each family bought an unblemished lamb at the Temple grounds. The sins of the family were laid on the lamb, and then the priests slaughtered it. Its blood was poured on the altar and the family's sins were washed away. Against this background, we see Jesus as the "Lamb of God, that takest away the sins of the world." The lamb was eaten at the Passover meal; Jesus' body, the bread, is broken and eaten as thanksgiving (in the Greek language, "eucharist"). He is the sacrifice. The cup of wine traditionally shared at the Passover meal as the "cup of affliction" becomes for the faithful the blood of Christ that cleanses and reconciles the people with God as no sacrificial lamb's blood can do. Moreover, Jesus' blood seals the new covenant as the blood of sacrificial animals sealed the old covenant between God and the Hebrew people. (See Exodus 24:8.)

One other important image needs to be understood. When Jesus says (Matt 26:29) "I tell you that I shall not drink again of this fruit of the vine until that day when I drink it new with you in my Father's kingdom," he is referring to the messianic banquet.

> On this mountain the Lord of hosts will make for all peoples a feast of fat things, a feast of wine on the lees, of fat things full of marrow, of wine on the lees well refined. And he will destroy on this mountain the covering that is cast over all peoples, the veil that is spread over all nations (Isaiah 25:6-7).

The Eucharist is a foretaste of that banquet. We step "into" the kingdom of God each time we share the Eucharist. We gather at the banquet table today knowing that, as we do so, we are getting our "first course" in the banquet that is to come. Moreover, we join at the Eucharist with all those who have gone before and sing one great triumphant hymn of praise, "with Angels, and Archangels and all the company of heaven" (BCP p. 362).

Week of the Sunday closest to July 20

The Old Testament readings:

The walls of Jericho came tumbling down as the army of Joshua marched around the city for the seventh straight day. Perhaps an earthquake hit the area, or a portion of the walls was torn down as the Israelites attacked the city. In either case, years of relating this crucial event shaped the scene. Whatever really happened, God's power was revealed that day. That is the point of telling the story from one generation to the next.

The Lord's command to destroy the inhabitants of Jericho, with the exception of Rahab and her family, needs to be understood in the light of how our biblical ancestors understood God's will at that time. Joshua understood his mission as conquest and destruction. He would understand a relationship with a god who would require total destruction; that is the way he would interpret revelations in dreams, inspirations, or from the sacred lots that were thrown to determine God's will. Israel's enemies would naturally be the enemies of God. It would be natural for him to understand that God would want total destruction of the city and its inhabitants. Though we may consider ourselves far more humane than our biblical ancestors, we have justified annihilating our enemies, with bombs, assuming that we, too, were exercising the will of God.

From joyful victory the story soon turns to humiliating defeat when a group of Joshua's men were defeated by the men of Ai. That loss was interpreted to be a sign that someone disobeyed the command of the Lord and kept valuable loot from the city rather than turning it over to the Lord's treasury. The defeat caused a crisis in faith on the part of the people and even for Joshua himself. When the guilty man was discovered and punished, victory against the city of Ai could be assured. Tuesday's reading describes the clever tactics of the Israelites that led to the defeat of the city.

Wednesday's reading describes a great covenant-making ceremony near Shechem. The Israelites stood facing each other with the Ark of the Covenant between them. Joshua read the blessings and the curses from the Torah. Skim over Deuteronomy 11:29-30 and 27:1 through 29:1 for a sense of what Joshua read to the people that day as they massed between Mt. Ebal and Mt. Gerizim. Perhaps the blessings and curses were recited from side to side in litany fashion. The people were reminded of their responsibilities in the new land as they became a settled people living among the Canaanites. The story served as a reminder to the Israelites of later generations that Israel had a destiny to live up to. Anything less than the following of God's will as revealed in Torah would lead to their ultimate defeat. When Israel was sent into foreign exile many years later, scenes such as the one described on Wednesday would be remembered.

"Sun, stand thou still at Gibeon, and thou Moon in the valley of Aijalon. 'And the sun stood still, and the moon stayed, until the nation took vengeance on their enemies'" (Joshua 10:12b-13). Joshua ordered the sun to stand still so that he could defeat the Amorite kings who attacked the Gibeonites. No possibility of a natural phenomenon such as an earthquake can explain this terrifying scene of God's power exercised on behalf of Israel. As this story was shared by storyteller and balladeer over the generations, details of God's intervention would take on miraculous proportions, becoming statements of praise and faith in a God who acted for Israel. Notice that one of the Amorite kings was from the city of Jerusalem. That strategic city was not taken by Israel until David became king years later.

We skip over some twelve chapters between Friday's and Saturday's readings. Those chapters describe the rest of the conquest of Canaan, and then detail the distribution of the conquered lands among the twelve tribes of Israel. The account is not accurate historically. As I just pointed out in connection with Jerusalem, not all of Canaan was conquered by Joshua and his army. Israel moved in with the Canaanites, taking some cities and leaving others to the inhabitants they found there. The twelve tribes may have settled in the general areas described in Joshua, but the exact boundaries of the tribal territories as described is highly questionable.

Our week closes with Joshua's farewell address to the people just before his death. It was a firm warning to stay close to the commands of the Torah. Israel must not become polluted with the practices of other peoples. Thus, intermarriage between Jew and gentile could not be condoned. A breaking of the provisions of the covenant, Joshua warned, would result in God's withdrawing blessings from the nation.

The second readings:

Paul's major concern in the readings we share this week is for Christian unity in the midst of diversity. One is not to judge the place another Christian is in. Some Christians will follow dietary laws that others do not, but what matters is their life in the Lord and not their outward acts of devotion. A nonjudgmental stance must inform the life of the Christian community. "Welcome one another, therefore, as Christ has welcomed you, for the glory of God" (Rom 15:7). *The New English Bible* uses the word "accept" in place of the RSV translation "welcome." Yet within the diversity of life, Christians must speak out with one voice to the glory of the Lord (Rom 15:6). Paul's hope was that individuals would focus their actions on the good of the whole community, a community that looked beyond itself to the Christ who empowered it in the Holy Spirit.

An Advent theme is set in Monday's reading. We must wake up as out of a sleep for the time of Christ's deliverance is approaching. Romans 13:8-14 is appointed for reading at the Eucharist on the First Sunday in Advent, Year A. The images of Advent are beautifully set forth in the text.

The Gospel readings:

This week in midsummer may feel like Holy Week to you as you read the familiar story of Jesus' betrayal, arrest and trial.

Matthew's account of Jesus' arrest and trial are taken from Mark's gospel. The description of Judas' death, assigned for reading on Friday, is unique to Matthew, however. Matthew based his description of Judas' death on a quotation from Zechariah 11:13. The gospel writer did not have his Hebrew scripture down perfectly in his mind, however. He ascribed the quotation to Jeremiah, rather than Zechariah! (Matt. 27:9.)

Week of the Sunday closest to July 27

The Old Testament readings:

Old Joshua felt his life drawing to a close. He called the twelve tribes of Israel together at a sacred place. Shechem had been one of the stopping points for Abraham and Sarah generations earlier as they entered the land of the Canaanites. Abraham had built an altar there as a remembrance that the Lord had appeared to him in a vision, promising the land to his descendants. Later, Jacob passed by Shechem and marked the place as holy.

Standing on this hallowed spot, Joshua rehearsed once again all the mighty acts that God had done for Israel. The victories achieved were not of the people's doing. The Lord had exercised power for the people, Joshua reminded them. Joshua concluded his rehearsal with a call to covenant: ". . .choose this day whom you will serve. . .as for me and my house, we will serve the Lord" (Joshua 24:15). The people cry out as with one voice that they, too, would serve the Lord and remain faithful.

From rehearsal and promise of covenant, Joshua turned to somber warning. The promise to enter into covenant with the Lord could not be taken lightly. If people turned from the Lord to worship the gods of the Canaanites and if they forgot the covenant in any way, then God would punish them severely. Joshua clearly doubted the good intentions of the people, made in the heat of the moment. He set up a great stone to be a "witness" of the covenant and as a reminder of the promise made there.

As Christians gather for the Holy Eucharist, a similar covenant renewal happens. With the hearing of scripture and with the rehearsal of the mighty acts of God in the prayer of consecration, God's presence in our history is remembered. The creed and the offering of ourselves at the offertory is our way of saying, "This day we choose." The bread and the cup become living witnesses of the covenant we know in Christ. The confession is a reminder that we, too, stray far from the covenant sealed with the cross.

The Book of Judges becomes the focus of study beginning Tuesday. This book continues the deuteronomic history of Israel begun with the books of Deuteronomy and Joshua and continuing through to the end of 2 Kings. We'll be looking at the period extending from about 1225 B.C. to 1025 B.C. as we read Judges.

The tribes moved into some areas of Canaan and settled down among the Canaanites. In some areas they held power. In other locations they did not.

The Israelites were a rough nomadic people. The Canaanites were a settled people accustomed to raising crops or living in a walled city. The Canaanites worshiped gods of field and hill top. Successful crops meant following the local rite and ritual at the local shrine. As Israel settled into the life of city or field, it was easy for them to adopt the religious customs of their neighbors. After all, a trip to the local shrine was a part of the method of planting and harvesting. It is easy to see how Israel's nomadic religious traditions were soon compromised.

The deuteronomic writers, working during and after the reign of King Josiah in the 7th century, wove stories together that had been told by word of mouth for generations. They also added their historical theological interpretation of the stories as well. The running theological commentary:

> . . .consists of four parts: (a)sin (sin of idolatry usually); (b)punishment (usually invasion by the surrounding nations); (c)repentance (usually expressed by the words "and they cried out to God," implying acknowledgment of sin and prayer for divine intervention); (d)liberation (God hears them by sending one of the judges to save and liberate them from their oppressors.*

Watch for this pattern in your reading in the coming weeks.

---

*Peter F. Ellis, *The Men and the Message of the Old Testament* (Collegeville, Minn.: The Liturgical Press), p. 190.

We see the pattern unfolding as we begin reading Judges on Tuesday. Israel had sinned by turning to the gods and ways of the Canaanites. The people cried out and Ehud, the first of the twelve judges of the book, appeared on the scene. Being left-handed, Ehud was able to draw his knife and kill the Moabite king who would have been immediately suspicious had Ehud reached with his right hand for the weapon.

"So Moab was subdued that day under the hand of Israel. And the land had rest for eighty years" (Judges 3:30). That refrain signaled completion of the four-fold cycle. Liberation had come and the people *momentarily* returned to the Lord. Deborah, the wife of Lappidoth, was the second judge. She was a charismatic leader who won her authority with words of power ascribed to the Lord. Barak, the military leader, wanted her to go along on the military campaign to which she had called him.

Though the lectionary reading on Thursday begins with Judges 4:4, I'd begin reading at the beginning of the chapter where the deuteronomic pattern is again apparent. Because of Israel's unfaithfulness, the Lord raised up Jabin, a Canaanite ruler, to harass the people. Sisera was Jabin's general. Another name to watch for on Thursday is Heber the Kenite. Heber had a loose tribal connection with the Israelites, but he was also allied with Jabin. Consequently Sisera thought it was safe to appear at Heber's tent for sanctuary. Though he may have been able to trust Heber, he could not trust Heber's wife, Jael, who promptly killed him, after lulling him into sleep.

Friday's and Saturday's reading is an ancient ballad that immortalizes the story of Deborah. The ballad offers us an insight into how stories were handed on in those times. Picture a balladeer appearing at the town gate and singing this ballad, accompanied by a stringed instrument. The people may have joined in the singing by offering a refrain at points in the ballad. Children must have been entranced by the ballad and they, in turn, would have sung it to their children, and so it was handed on until finally put into writing by the deuteronomic editors.

The second readings:

We'll conclude our six weeks in the Epistle to the Romans on Tuesday with a long list of people whom Paul wanted to commend to the church in Rome, and with a final warning to avoid heretics who stir up discord in the church. The letter concludes with an extended doxology.

On Wednesday the Book of Acts of the Apostles becomes our focus. Acts is really book two of the Gospel of Luke. The same author wrote both, though they are separated in the New Testament by the Gospel of John. Where the Gospel of Luke relates the good news of Jesus Christ, Acts proclaims the good news of the Holy Spirit empowering the church to carry on the work of the risen Christ. The book would have been written at about the same time as the Gospel of Luke, from around 75 to 85 A.D. It was written for educated Greeks familiar with the historic style of the time. The author of Luke/Acts wanted to make clear that the Christian need not wait for the return of Christ at the end of the age to proclaim the reign of God. Christ had empowered the church with the Holy Spirit. In a real sense, Christ had risen within the church and his continuing activity in creation and history would be made known through that church.

After the ascension of Jesus, reported in Acts 1, the gift of the Holy Spirit came to the apostles as they gathered on the Jewish feast of Pentecost. That feast remembers the giving of the covenant to Moses on Mt. Sinai. It remains a major Jewish festival to this day. Read Exodus 19:14-16 for a description of the thunder and lightning that shook the mountain when Moses prepared to receive the covenant. This imagery was used poetically by the writer of Luke/Acts as he described the receiving of the Holy Spirit. This moment marks the giving of a new covenant, or testament, to the peoples of the world, one not written on stone, but "written on the hearts of the people," as Jeremiah had said (Jer 31:33). The tongues spoken by the apostles were not ecstatic tongues of praise, but were the tongues of every known language in the world. The covenant made known through the Holy Spirit is one that will be understood and received by all nations and not just by the Jews.

Peter's sermon would not have been recorded word for word. The several sermons ascribed to Peter and Paul in Acts were reconstructions by Luke, based on the proclamation of the good news that the church was making at the time.

The Hebrew scripture, especially the psalms, furnished proof texts for the Christian evangelists. Saturday's reading contains two quotations from the Book of Psalms, words ascribed to King David, though authorship of those psalms is unknown. Jesus is the one who comes to fulfill the words written long ago, Luke wanted to point out. The Christian evangelists and the writers of the gospels often took their quotations from Hebrew scripture out of context, but they saw in those words entirely new meaning in the light of Jesus' death and resurrection.

The Gospel readings:
We will complete our reading of the Gospel of Matthew this week. The trial, crucifixion, death and resurrection of Jesus draw attention in the final section. The familiar scene of Pilate washing his hands is unique to Matthew. At the time the gospel was written Christians were experiencing their first strong rejection by the Jewish hierarchy. The awful details of the Jews accepting guilt on themselves and future generations for Jesus' death need to be read in the light of the growing hatred between the church and the Jewish community at the time the gospel was written. These words have led to generations of persecution for the Jews at the hands of Christians, culminating in the holocaust in Nazi Germany.

Jesus was placed on the cross at nine in the morning, a detail recorded by Mark, but not included in Matthew's account. From noon until three in the afternoon, darkness came over the land. When Jesus died at 3:00, he had been on the cross for six hours, a shorter time than normal. The flogging, or whipping, before crucifixion was a cruel introduction to the process of dying.

The practice of three hours of prayer and meditation on Good Friday comes from the tradition of the three hours of darkness. Christians keep the watch with the faithful women who gathered at the cross at the time of Jesus' death. Some of Matthew's details of what happened when Jesus died need to be read with a poet's eye, for Matthew drew motifs and details from Old Testament writings to heighten the impact of Jesus' death.

The week ends appropriately with Jesus' great commission to the disciples to go forth into the world baptizing in the name of the Trinity and "...teaching them to observe all that I have commanded you; and lo, I am with you always, to the close of the age" (Matt 28:20).

Week of the Sunday closest to August 3

The Old Testament readings:

Gideon, the third of the judges, is the important figure of study this week. The deuteronomist's statement of Israel's decadence lets us know that we are beginning another cycle of despair followed by repentance and salvation. "The people of Israel did what was evil in the sight of the Lord; and the Lord gave them into the hand of Midian seven years" (Judges 6:1). Gideon, the least of the sons of Joash who headed the least of the families of the tribe of Manasseh, had a vision of the Lord who appeared to him by a terebinth tree at Ophrah.

Like Moses before him, this least of the sons of Joash needed proof that it was really the Lord who had approached him in his vision. Gideon's offering was consumed by fire and later a fleece of wool was used as a further means of testing the truth of the vision. Satisfied of the validity of his calling, Gideon made his first move to establish authority amongst his clansmen by tearing down the altar to the local diety. Gideon called together the tribes of Asher, Zebulun and Naphtali. The judges were not national leaders, but charismatic leaders who in a time of crisis would call together various tribes to help put down the enemy. We see this pattern in Monday's reading.

The Lord wanted Israel to remember that it was by God's hand that Israel was saved and not by its own strength. A group of 300 men going to battle with torches, jars, and trumpets and defeating a huge force would show God's power. Three hundred men who "lap the water like dogs" are to be the mighty army of Gideon!

The battle was won when the Midianites, awakened from sleep by 300 screaming men blowing trumpets and smashing jugs, fought each other and fled in panic. This account, including the details of a strange dream described by one of the Midanites, may well have been shared in the form of a ballad such as Deborah's Song. The details of the frightened Midianites fleeing at the hand of Gideon's screaming band of followers would have brought amusement to many generations.

The tribe of Ephraim was called out by Gideon in a second alarm as he pursued the Midianites. The fact that they were not mustered for the initial battle angered the Ephraimites. Gideon quickly placated them with a reminder of the important role they played by capturing Oreb and Zeeb.

Succoth and Penuel were cities east of the Jordan settled by the tribe of Gad. Moses had been concerned that those eastern tribes would not support the tribes west of the Jordan, and his worry was well placed. (See Num 32.) When Gideon asked for assistance for his weary men, he received only sarcasm. "You'll never capture Zebah and Zalmunna. Why should we bother to help you?" Gideon did capture the two kings and later returned to Succoth and Penuel and punished the people for their lack of assistance.

We leave Gideon Thursday. Though he refused to be king at the request of the tribes, he did allow a golden ephod to be made, clearly a violation of Israel's covenant with the Lord. What a tragic end to this great story. Visions of the Lord forgotten, Gideon encouraged an act of sin among the people that would serve to draw their attention away from the mighty acts of God. Paddy Chayefsky in his play, *Gideon*, placed this statement on the lips of the angel of God:

> God no more believes it odd that man cannot believe in God. Man believes the best he can, which means, it seems, belief in man. Then let him don my gold ephod and let him be a proper god. Well, let him try it anyway.*

Gideon's son, Abimelech, commands our attention for the balance of the week. Since his mother had been a citizen of Shechem (a city still in the hands of Canaanites), he saw an opportunity to consolidate power and authority as king. Beth-Millo, mentioned in Friday's reading, was a section of the city of Shechem. Abimelech's brother, Jotham, was able to take the

*Paddy Chayefsky, *Gideon* (Carnegie Productions, Inc. 1961), pp. 137-138.

steam out of the uprising with the recitation of a fable offered in the hearing of the citizens of Shechem. The good trees (Gideon) wouldn't consider being king of Shechem or Israel. Only the worthless thorn bush (Abimelech) would consider such a thing. But to take shelter under the thorn bush would also lay one open to the destructive fire so often associated with their growth.

Shechem went against Abimelech who was later killed in a battle to take the city of Thebez. A king was not to rule the tribes of Israel, at least not in this generation. God must be the only king for Israel.

The second readings:

The outline of early Christian communal life must still shape our vision of Christian community today. The people gathered to hear the teaching of the apostles, to share fellowship, to "break bread" (celebrate the Eucharist), and to pray. Out of their common life, shared in the power of the Holy Spirit, came acts of power that amazed the surrounding community. Everything was shared in common so that each person had what was needed. The early Christians were all Jewish so that the Temple was still a major focus in their lives; they would also gather in private homes for the breaking of bread.

Peter began to show a power of healing like Jesus', providing Peter with another opportunity to proclaim Christ's resurrection. Notice a pattern of narrative developed by the writer of Luke/Acts to describe the early ministry of the apostles. First came an event in which God's power was shown. Then came a reflection of that event in the preaching of Peter, ending with a call by Peter for the people to repent (meaning to change or turn in a new direction) and accept Christ as Savior. New converts came into fellowship at each occasion of preaching.

This pattern must also serve as a model for the church as it continues to function in history. We point to the acts of God evidenced in our time as the starting point for reflection and as the central point for repentance and conversion.

Peter's preaching led to the first arrest of the Christians, but the arrest led only to an opportunity to preach before the court. A theme throughout Acts is that nothing can stop the work of the Holy Spirit. Arrest, suffering, persecution only led to the further spreading of the gospel.

Saturday's reading repeats the picture of communal life in the primitive Christian church, fulfilling the call of the Torah that no one shall be poor (Deut 15:4). The story of Ananias and Sapphira, who lied to the apostles and held back the proceeds of the sale of their property, was a story told in the primitive church to emphasize the standards of Christian community.

The Gospel readings:

Though John followed the pattern of the synoptic gospels (Matthew, Mark and Luke) in recording the events of Jesus' life, death and resurrection, he departed radically in giving the reader a theological interpretation of those events, rather than in proclaiming them. John assumed that his readers knew what Jesus had said and done. John used poetry, metaphor and symbolic language to write his theological statement of the Christ, as one must when dealing with ultimate mystery. As you read the long and intricate speeches of Jesus in this gospel, realize that you are reading beautiful poetry that leads the Christian to an understanding of what stands behind the words and actions of Jesus.

The opening words of John serve as an overture, setting forth the theme and message of the gospel. The Word, or Wisdom, of God that has always existed came to men and women in the flesh of the man, Jesus. In Jesus, God reached out of eternity so that people could know God intimately and personally. Later in the gospel the powerful news is carried further; through the Holy Spirit, the incarnate experience of God continues, for God comes to each succeeding generation "in the flesh" of human encounter to touch men and women personally with continuing revelation. God still dwells with us!

John the Baptist pointed beyond himself to Jesus, and at least two of John's disciples turned from John to Jesus. One of those disciples was the brother of Simon Peter. The Gospel of John often differs in its account of events from the synoptic gospels. Matthew, Mark and Luke reported that Jesus called Peter as he saw Peter at his fishing boat. In the Gospel of John, however, it was Peter's brother who brought Peter to see Jesus. John may have inherited different traditions about Jesus. In other cases, he may have altered the stories to express his theological concerns.

The term, "lamb of God," appears in Wednesday's lection. The title comes out of the Temple ritual.

Exodus 12 directs that an unblemished lamb be slaughtered at the Passover and consumed by the people. Lambs were also offered in sacrifice at other festival days at the Temple. The offering of the innocent lamb at Passover was seen as a way of becoming at-one with God again after the separation that the people had caused by their sinfulness. The sacrifice of the Paschal or Passover Lamb restored the people to God. The Passover was a pilgrim festival; persons came from all over the nation to share this feast in Jerusalem. They would enter the city and then go to the Temple, where they would often buy a lamb from the sellers at the Temple grounds. The Lamb was then offered in sacrifice. After the blood was sprinkled on the altar, the people would take the meat to their rented rooms, where it would be cooked and eaten as a part of the Passover meal.

. . . (Jesus) then offered himself as "a perfect sacrifice for the whole world." (prayer of consecration, BCP, p.362) The disciples came to realize that Jesus was the true Paschal Lamb that takes away the sins of the people by the forgiving love of God that he showed forth from the cross and at the resurrection.**

**Joseph P. Russell, *Sharing Our Biblical Story* (Minneapolis, Minn.: Winston Press, 1979), pp. 151-152

Week of the Sunday closest to August 10

The Old Testament readings:
This week we continue our reading of the Book of Judges. To understand the rather strange stories, place yourself in the eleventh century before Christ. Our biblical ancestors were attempting to hold on to their tribal lands while being attacked on all sides by various nations and tribes. The stories come from this time of struggle. We deal here with folk tale and legend, as well as with historic incidents. The stories express the conviction that the God who saved Israel from Egyptian oppression is the same God who works in history to defeat the Ammonites, the Philistines, and other enemies.

On Monday and Tuesday, Jephthah, the judge, is our focus. Though in his youth he had been rejected because he was the son of an alien woman, Jephthah was chosen by his tribesmen to lead them in battle against the Ammonites. His vow of human sacrifice was not unusual for his time. Such sacrifice was an accepted practice among the surrounding peoples, and the custom found its way into Hebrew life as well. The fact that Jephthah's daughter was the first to greet her father from the door of his house heightens the pathos of the story.

What appears to be a strange war between Ephraim and Gilead in chapter 12 may have been a limited family feud rather than a major confrontation between tribes. Notice the password, "Shibboleth," used by the men of Gilead. The Ephraimites could not pronounce the word correctly because of their accents. Thus the word served as a test to separate friend from foe. The word has been taken into the English language to mean "password" or "slogan," for example, "That motto has become their Shibboleth in this convention."

On Tuesday through Thursday we read the early accounts of the judge, Samson. These are legendary tales told by our biblical ancestors as a way of belittling the despised Philistines. Though the stories may sound harsh to our ears, they provided laughter for the Israelites at the expense of the enemy.

The second readings:

The Book of Acts continues to be our focus for the second reading this week. The center of Christian activity remained in Jerusalem, but the opposition to the followers of Jesus was heightened as the power of the Holy Spirit was seen more strongly in the lives of the apostles. Luke's intention is to show the increasing opposition of the Jews and to point out how impossible it was to stop the activity of the Holy Spirit. Even prison could not hold back the apostles from proclaiming the gospel in word and act.

In chapter 6 we are introduced to the Greek-speaking deacons, specifically to Stephen, the first Christian martyr. Notice the custom of the laying on of hands for passing on the authority and power of the Holy Spirit. We also see the origin of the order of deacons.

The Gospel readings:

Some familiar passages from the Gospel of John will be read this week. On Monday we read of a rather strange conversation between Jesus and Nicodemus, held "by night," showing the need for secrecy and symbolic of coming out of darkness into light. We see here a pattern in John's writing: Jesus talks with someone at a metaphorical level. The person hears Jesus' words literally and fails to understand. The gospel writer then has Jesus explain the metaphor in an extended theological discourse. This is the Fourth Gospel writer's method of expressing, in beautiful poetic terms, the theology of Christ's ministry.

Notice on Wednesday and Thursday this same pattern is followed as Jesus encounters the woman at the well. The living water Jesus refers to is not indoor plumbing as the woman imagines, but a relationship with the Lord revealed through Jesus Christ!

The cure of the nobleman's son, read on Friday, is the second of seven signs in the gospel. Each sign is a further indication of Jesus' nature. To know Jesus is to experience eternal life, we read in John 17:3, and that life was happening as people grew to know Jesus in the signs of his love and power.

The third sign of Jesus is the cure of the sick man at the Pool of Bethesda, read on Saturday. Notice again the pattern of dialogue that grows out of the healing act. For a clearer understanding of the Gospel of John, read the discourses of Jesus as poetic statements of theology, rather than as literal accounts of speeches of Jesus.

Week of the Sunday closest to August 17

The Old Testament readings:

We conclude our reading of the Book of Judges Wednesday and begin reading the Book of Job. (Chapters 19-21 in the Judges are not designated for reading in the daily lectionary.)

Our story in Judges 17 and 18 is a confusing one because of several editorial changes and additions made over the years. Again, remember that these are ancient campfire-type folk stories that explain the origins of customs, sanctuaries or animosities between tribes and nations. The violence and injustice reflect the pressures and ideas of the time, and also show the hand of the tribal storyteller shaping the material, both to hold the attention of the listener and to pass on tradition to the next generation.

An outline of the story may help you understand the action. Micayehu, or Micah, had stolen money from his mother. By promising to return it and use the money for sacred purposes, he received a blessing rather than a curse from his mother. He made carved sacred images from the coins he had taken and then hired a Levite priest to look after the shrine he had created. The comment in Judges 17:6 explains these loose practices by pointing out that ". . .there was no king in Israel; every man did what was right in his own eyes." Meanwhile, the tribe of Dan needed a new territory for permanent settlement, and five men went out from the tribe to scout for possible alternatives. With six hundred additional men, the tribe of Dan took the undefended territory around the city of Laish. The Levite priest of Micah and the idols created by him were removed by the Danites to their new city which was renamed Dan. From that time until the captivity of Israel in 721 B.C., the city of Dan was an important shrine for the northern kingdom.

On Thursday we begin reading Job, a dramatic "Wisdom" poem written during or after the Babylonian exile. Thursday's and Friday's selections set the scene for the poem that follows by telling the story of Job and his great misfortune.

The second readings:

Our reading of Acts continues with the conclusion of the story of Stephen. His martyrdom introduces a new person to the scene: "And Saul was consenting to his death." The impact of Saul's later conversion is heightened by this brief sentence of grim introduction.

Watch for another dramatic turn in the narrative Tuesday. Persecutions in Jerusalem forced the Christians there out into the surrounding country. As a direct result of the persecution, the Christian movement was spread further! Nothing can thwart the purposes of God, the writer of Acts makes clear. The very measures used against the church are the measures that lead to its growth.

We met Philip last week. He was one of the seven deacons set aside to minister to the widows. Now his healing and preaching ministry begins to lead some of the Samaritan people to conversion. Peter and John confirm Philip's ministry by laying hands on his converts, at which time they receive the Holy Spirit. A sense of apostolic authority is contained in Wednesday's reading, along with the reminder of the power of the Holy Spirit revealed in the life of the church. Eunuchs and Samaritans were considered outcasts by the Jews. Their conversion is a radical statement of acceptance into the church of those who had been outcasts.

The week's reading of Acts is rounded off with the dramatic story of Saul's conversion on the road to Damascus.

The Gospel readings:

Monday's and Tuesday's readings are John's theological interpretation of Jesus' healing at the pool of Bethesda. Read this as a theological discourse on the relationship between Jesus and God the Father. God's life-giving power is revealed through the Son. To listen to the Son is to hear the Father. To accept Jesus as the Son of God is to receive the eternal life offered by God the Father. Jesus is the source of life because God the Father is the ultimate source of life (v. 26). To reject Jesus is to reject

God. These words of judgment close the discourse aimed at those who doubted the authority of the healing act they had just seen.

The balance of this week is spent reflecting on the metaphor of Jesus as the "bread of life." Notice again the pattern of an act of Jesus followed by misunderstanding and extended explanation. In this case we have the miracle of the loaves, followed immediately by Jesus walking on water. Look for the real bread of life, the bread that lasts, the bread that is Jesus, the living Christ.

Week of the Sunday closest to August 24

The Old Testament readings:

We'll be reading the Book of Job for the next four weeks. It belongs to a type of biblical writing called "wisdom literature." Unlike most of the biblical writings that deal with Israel's history from the perspective of the covenant relationship between God and the people, wisdom literature looks at the individual's relationship with God. Wisdom literature rises above all historical context and touches every person in every age. Job is the book of each one of us. Though Job is often associated with the question of suffering or the need for patience, the primary focus of this great literary work is the individual's relationship with God. What can we know of God, and what is our relationship with the Creator, are the questions of Job.

The writer of Job took an ancient folk tale common not only to Hebrew tradition, but to surrounding peoples as well. The good man is tested by God to see how strong his faith really is. The writer inserted his beautiful wisdom poem, with the speeches of Job given in answer to the speeches of his so-called friends who raised all the orthodox arguments of Judaism to convince Job that he had sinned and his suffering had come as punishment. Job insisted on his innocence. His anger at God grew stronger as he realized he must deal with an unseen, unknown adversary whose seemingly unjust actions could never be comprehended by a mere mortal. The Book of Ecclesiastes is another example of wisdom literature in the Bible that deals with much the same issue. "What can we know of the Creator's will for us?"

The voice from the whirlwind is the answer of the unseen, unknown God. Beginning with chapter 38, we read the Lord's response. No explanation of Job's suffering is given. Instead, Job discovers a relationship based on total trust and surrender to the deepest creative mystery of existence that is God, rather than on the stilted merit-matched-by-reward understanding of orthodox Judaism of the time. From this relationship comes a living relationship with God, a relationship that can lead to worship, praise, and trust in the face of life's unanswered questions.

This week we'll read parts of the first round of arguments between Job and his "comforters." The stage is set for confrontation between Job and the three friends and between Job and the unseen God.

The second readings:

Acts this week reads like a serialized adventure story. Saul's sudden conversion was met at first by suspicion and then by excitement in the church. The hostility of the Jews sent Paul out of the city to Tarsus, his home, and our attention turns once more to the apostle Peter, sent by a vision to gentile peoples for the first time. The power of the gospel walks through prison doors, overcomes persecution, and bridges seemingly impossible gulfs of long-standing prejudice and rejection.

The Gospel readings:

Monday we conclude the discourse about Jesus as the bread of life. The reading has definite eucharistic overtones: "...he who eats my flesh and drinks my blood has eternal life..." (John 6:54a). Some scholars feel that John 6:51-58 was originally part of the Last Supper narrative in chapter 13 and later was moved to this position to enlarge on the theme of Jesus as the bread of life. Indeed, the whole chapter could have formed the basis for a Christian Passover celebration, using the feeding narrative and following discourse as an important part of the sacred meal.* In any case, the chapter provides a beautiful sacramental statement of the Eucharist. Read it with The Book of Common Prayer open beside your Bible, comparing the great thanksgiving of the Eucharist with the words from the Gospel of John (BCP, pp. 362-363, 368-375; Lutheran Book of Worship, 207ff, 244ff, 28ff).

---

*Raymond E. Brown, *Gospel of John, Anchor Bible.* Garden City, New York: Doubleday and Company, 1979; pp. 295-303

The readings for Wednesday through Friday, taken from chapter 7, again deal with the direct relationship between Jesus and God the Father. The chapter also shows the increasing hostility toward Jesus. Though some believe, more refuse to believe despite all the signs of Jesus' power and love. Even his own brothers do not have faith in him.

On Saturday we move to another metaphor that helps to describe the role of Jesus in the world. "I am the light of the world. . ." we read in John 8:12. Anyone who follows Jesus will be walking in the light that comes directly from God.

Week of the Sunday closest to August 31

The Old Testament readings:

We will continue to read portions of the first round of speeches from Job's friends, along with his rebuttal to each speech, until Thursday when we'll move into the second and third round of speeches and rebuttals. Each series moves more deeply into the typical arguments that come out of Jewish orthodoxy, with profoundly moving denials of that orthodox response by Job.

Realize, as you read, that this is a radical work for its time and equally radical for our day. All the pat answers of orthodox faith are held up to question. How many of us feel that we have earned our relationship with God? "Why, I'm a cradle Episcopalian and spirit-filled at that," we say with some degree of pride. "The Lord has certainly blessed me since my conversion with a good job and a happy family life." But then, something comes into our life that seems to contradict the blessing. "What have I done to deserve this?" we may say at such a time.

Look for familiar words in Friday's reading: "For I know that my Redeemer lives. . ." (Job 19:25a). You may recognize those words from the burial office, as it is one of the options chosen for reading at the time of death. Someday, Job believed, one would stand up for him before God, like a defense attorney standing before the judge and jury in a court of law. The Redeemer would stand by Job and, at last, Job would be justified before the Lord.

The second readings:

Our adventure stories from the Book of Acts of the Apostles continue this week, giving us a running account of the inevitable spread of the church in the Mediterranean world. More gentile Greeks were converted at Antioch, and we learn that it was in this church that the followers of Christ were first called Christians. The scene shifts once more to Peter and his second miraculous escape from prison. Notice how often imprisonment figures in the lives of the apostles. To be a Christian is to face the power structures of the age, no matter when we live. These stories should remind us to look in the prisons of our own time. We, too, may be persecuting the Word of God as it is enfleshed in the issues of the twentieth century. The Word of God is a radical word, calling into question all our assumptions about our society and life.

Thursday we begin a new part of the adventure of Paul (Saul). He and Barnabas were set aside by the laying on of hands for a new work and sent on the first of Paul's three missionary journeys. You'll need a map of the missionary journeys of Paul in your lap as you read from Acts from now until the middle of October. Paul's epistles will take on a new interest for you if you can locate the actual cities in which he spent time. As you read about the churches he established, turn to the letters (epistles) he wrote to those churches.

The Gospel readings:
Monday through Wednesday is a continuation of last week's dialogue with the unbelieving Jews. Jesus' words are blunt and confrontational in the verses assigned for these days. Though there is no doubt that Jesus confronted the Jews with strong words, the words we read here are most likely statements of the early church directed toward the Jews of the second century and written to encourage the new gentile Christians. The Jews had rejected the Christ, and, therefore, the promise was now passed on to those who could accept the signs of Jesus and become his followers. To live in the truth that Jesus brings is to be a free person, in contrast to living under the enslavement of sin. The Jews argued that their relationship of freedom with God was guaranteed because they were children of the Mosaic Covenant. Jesus' words echo John the Baptist's statement in Matthew 3:9b. ". . .God is able from these stones to raise up children to Abraham," John had said. The writer points out that one's relationship to God is really judged by one's actions, in this case the necessary action of love for Jesus and faith that he, indeed, was the Son of God. Incidentally, Jesus' frequent use of the words "I am. . ." to identify himself was a play on

the mysterious name of God revealed to Moses in Exodus 3:14: "I AM WHO I AM...I AM has sent me to you." When Jesus said he was "I am," he meant that he himself was God. No wonder the Jews picked up stones to throw at him! (John 8:59)

On Thursday and Friday we read of the sixth sign of Jesus, the healing of the man born blind. This act becomes the opportunity for the writer to reflect on Jesus as the "light of the world." To know Jesus and to accept him as Son of God is truly to see. We are judged if we think we can see without faith in Jesus.

Our week with John closes with the metaphor of Jesus as the good shepherd. Well known words of faith are found in verse 10:10b: "...I came that they may have life, and have it abundantly."

Week of the Sunday closest to September 7

The Old Testament readings:

On Sunday we are given one sampling from the third series of speeches between Job and his friends before moving on Monday to sample a portion of the speech of Elihu. Some scholars feel this speech was a later insertion by editors who feared the radical words of the poem and wanted to soften the impact. Elihu's speech runs from chapter 32 through 37. You may want to read the entire section and see if you agree. Look at 32:7-8 for a reminder that true wisdom comes from God's inspiration (or spirit?), not with age.

Tuesday through Friday we go back a few chapters and pick up Job's concluding monologue. If this were a court case, we would say that this is Job's closing defense argument. The first of the speeches of God is read on Saturday, a fitting way to begin your weekend! This is a magnificent statement of God's omnipotence. No person can possibly know the designs of God. "Have you commanded the morning since your days began, and caused the dawn to know its place...?" we read in Job 38:12. To presume to raise questions of God's justice or wisdom is to presume that we can understand what is past comprehension. Since Saturday is the Jewish sabbath and traditionally a time to reflect on the wonder of God's creation, this reading is particularly appropriate. Canticle 12, appointed for Saturday morning, gives thanks and praise for the creative power of God. See, also, the collect for Saturday on page 99 in The Book of Common Prayer and canticle 10 for Morning Prayer, which states in no uncertain terms that ". . . my thoughts are not your thoughts, nor your ways my ways. . ." (taken from Isaiah 55:6-11).

The second readings:

The readings for Monday through Wednesday continue the account of Paul's and Barnabas' first missionary journey. Increasing hostility of the Jews becomes a greater and greater problem as they travel. The pattern is set on this first journey. Paul arrived in each town and went first to the synagogue in an attempt to relate to the Jewish people. Sometimes he would be welcomed and even asked to talk to the synagogue community. The more he talked, however, the more radical his words were perceived. Acceptance turned to rejection, and Paul turned from Jew to gentile, going out into the larger community. As the gentiles were converted, Paul carefully trained elders to carry on the teaching and work of the church. When Paul left, the church carried on with the leadership he had prepared.

Beginning Thursday, we read about the controversy over Paul's and Barnabas' work in the early church. It was the understanding of the Jews who had converted to Christianity that one must be fully a Jew to become a follower of Christ. Not so, said Paul and others. There was no need to follow the letter of the Mosaic Convenant to become a Christian. To follow the covenant fully would have meant circumcision for all male converts, along with the strict dietary laws for everyone in the church. The first council of the church was called at Jerusalem where Paul and Barnabas gave an accounting of their activities among the gentiles and received the apostles' directive through James, the brother of Jesus.

The Gospel readings:
The "good shepherd" discourse continues Monday and Tuesday. Opposition from the Jews leads again to an attempt to stone Jesus. Stoning was the penalty under Mosaic law for the sin of blasphemy. Notice how many times the Jews tried to stone Jesus and look for the words that would have led them to such an act. Jesus claimed to be one with the Father, according to the writer of John.

Wednesday we turn to the seventh and final sign of Jesus, the raising of Lazarus. This act leads to Jesus' powerful statement, "I am the resurrection...". This final sign is a physical carrying out of Jesus' words in John 5:28, "...for the hour is coming when all who are in the tombs will hear his voice and come forth...". The event points to the full meaning of Jesus' life. This is not a resurrection because Lazarus still faced death, but the story serves to dramatize the theological statements the writer of John has been making in the preceding chapters.

Week of the Sunday closest to September 14

The Old Testament readings:

Our reading in the Book of Job is concluded Thursday. During the first part of the week we read the continuation of the Lord's response to Job. Remember that this is poetry. The writer is a skillful artist with words. He paints a picture of creation and weaves within that picture the reality that it is God who is the source of all creation, not man and woman. We can only respond in total awe to the total mystery as Job does in the reading appointed for Wednesday. Read Psalms 104 and 147 for a comparable poetic statement of God's creative power. We close our study of Job with the reading of chapter 28. It may seem odd to go back into the book after reading it to the end, but chapter 28 is a poetic hymn praising wisdom, an appropriate ending of our journey. Seeking wisdom is a part of being human, and ultimate wisdom is awe of God and the avoidance of evil.

Friday we turn to the Book of Esther for just one week. Esther has more value for understanding the feelings of the Jews in the time of the Greek domination than it does for theological insight. This is a story long on revenge and vindication and short on belief in God's mercy and salvation for all peoples. Still, it is well worth reading for it tells of our biblical history and roots. It also may satisfy our desire for the story to come out just right, in human terms. We want the bad people to get it in the end and the good folk to win out. Esther is that kind of story. The origin of Esther may lie in the need to provide a story that justifies celebrating Purim, a rather rowdy festival that could have entered Jewish tradition from surrounding cultures. Purim celebrants are directed by the Talmud ". . .to drink until they can no longer distinguish between 'cursed by Haman' and 'blessed by Mordecai'. . .'"*. So read this book as an ancient story shared by our biblical ancestors in times of persecution and struggle. Out of this narrative came the practices of a festival that proclaims hope and new possibilities in the

---

*The Interpreter's Dictionary of the Bible, vol. 3

face of injustices and oppression. If the story seems more than a little vindictive, realize that we all dream of revenge at some time. This book must always be read within the context of the whole Bible, where prophet and poet speak of God's loving grace for friend and foe alike.

The second readings:

This week in our reading of Acts we find Paul embarking on his second missionary journey with a new partner, Silas. As you read of Paul's journey to Philippi, follow his route on a New Testament map and read his letter to the Philippians to get more of a feel for Paul's life with the people there. Friday we move with Paul to Thessalonika, and you may want to read Paul's two letters to the Thessalonians as background. We leave Paul in Athens at the end of the week, realizing that Paul often met with failure as well as success in his missionary endeavors.

The Gospel readings:

Monday's gospel reading leads to a major turning point in the Gospel of John. Jesus entered Jerusalem the final time and prepared to face the death he knew awaited him. The anointing at Bethany seems a fitting preparation, since bodies were anointed for their burial. (See John 12:7.)

There is a Holy Week feeling as we read these passages. John 12:1-11 is assigned for the Monday in Holy Week in the eucharistic lectionary, and the account of Jesus entering Jerusalem turns our thoughts to Palm Sunday. Wednesday's reading is a statement of the meaning not only of Jesus' death, but of our own as well: ". . .unless a grain of wheat falls into the earth and dies, it remains alone, but if it dies, it bears much fruit" (John 12:24). These scenes in Jerusalem offer the writer of the gospel an opportunity again to express the theological implications of Jesus' life, death, and resurrection. Jesus is the light that comes into the world. Do we dare choose to live in darkness when the light has come? The last half of chapter 12 echoes the opening words of the gospel, but with a new significance as we move with Jesus into his final struggle.

Week of the Sunday closest to September 21

The Old Testament readings:

From Sunday through Friday, we'll be sharing the adventures of Esther and Mordecai. See if the story reminds you of others you've read from ancient literary sources. Our biblical ancestors were influenced by their surrounding cultures but, as they assimilated the literature and customs of other peoples, they shaped those traditions into their own understanding of how God was calling them into proclaiming his glory in the world. The victory of Esther and Mordecai was not just their victory over evil. It was God's victory over oppression. This is the message that strengthens Jew and Christian alike in this present age of oppression and continuing holocaust.

Saturday we begin reading of the prophet, Hosea. Hosea felt called by God to marry a prostitute, a woman who was bound to be unfaithful to him. Out of his experience would come a dramatic realization of how God felt toward his beloved nation, Israel. The people of God were as unfaithful as Gomer, the prostitute, was to Hosea, and yet the Lord could forgive that unfaithful people and take them back as his bride again.

The second readings:

Monday we enter the city of Corinth with Paul. I'd suggest reading through 1 and 2 Corinthians as a background study of this era in Paul's life. The church in Corinth presented a great many problems to the apostle. You can feel his frustration and anger as you read the letters.

Acts 18 gives us a thumbnail sketch of Paul's missionary method. Notice that he joined with others in Corinth who followed his trade of tentmaking and worked to support himself. This is the origin of the term, "tentmaking ministry," describing ordained deacons and priests who earn their income from work outside the church. Paul then preached to the Jews within the synagogue community. After being rejected there, he moved right next door to begin his work among the gentiles. Is it any wonder that Paul was roundly hated by the Jews in the towns where he worked? Lest we condemn the Jews of Paul's time, we need to put ourselves in their shoes. Picture someone coming into your congregation preaching a very radical message that seemed to go against the grain of much that you had been taught in church. Then think about this person setting up shop next door and attracting large numbers of people you consider as outcasts. Can you see yourself calling the police the first time the rowdy group next door raised their voices in strange hymns of praise?

Midweek we move with Paul back to Antioch (Acts 18:22-23) where he set out on his third missionary journey, which included major work in the city of Ephesus.

The Gospel readings:

This week we move from the Gospel of John to the Gospel of Luke. The remaining nine chapters of John are read at other times during the church year.

Luke presents a very different rendition of the good news than John. Luke was written for a gentile audience in about 85 A.D.. It is one of the three so-called synoptic gospels, meaning gospels written "through the same eye," or from the same perspective. Matthew, Mark and Luke contain many of the same events and sayings of Jesus, though each one follows a different approach and is aimed at a different audience.

Luke's major concern is to point out the universal nature of the good news. Jesus has come so that all people may know the salvation of the Lord. Luke shows a particular concern for the poor and the oppressed. Watch for it as you read each day. For example, look at Luke 1:51-53. "He has shown strength with his arm, he has scattered the proud in the imagination of their hearts, he has put down the mighty from their thrones, and exalted those of low degree; he has filled the hungry with good things, and the rich he has sent empty away." While Matthew talks about the "poor in spirit" being blessed (5:3), Luke gives no such modification to the happiness of the poor in the sight of the Lord: "Blessed are you poor, for yours is the kingdom of God" (Luke 6:20b). In Luke the rich who rely on their own strength and power are cursed: "But woe to you that are rich, for you have received your consolation" (Luke 6:24). These radical statements must be seen not just as statements of personal piety, but as prophetic utterances of political and social justice that comes through the working of the Holy Spirit. We are so familiar with the gospels that we tend not really to hear them.

The writer of Luke points up the work of the Holy Spirit in ways that Matthew and Mark do not. It is the Holy Spirit that empowers the disciples of Jesus to carry on the ministry, to proclaim the coming of the kingdom, to heal, and to teach.

Through this gospel we also learn the extent of God's forgiveness for us sinners. The parable of the prodigal son dramatizes the gospel of forgiveness and restoration. Luke alone offers it.

Read Luke with the understanding that it is the first of a two-part work. The Book of Acts of the Apostles is the second half of Luke's gospel, though separated in the New Testament by the Gospel of John. Luke's gospel gives us the universal message of salvation and healing as revealed through Jesus. In Acts that message is carried out by the church, empowered by the Holy Spirit. The apostles discover they have Jesus' power of healing and proclamation, for the risen Christ dwells within them through the Holy Spirit. The church, the gathered followers of Jesus, goes out to the gentile world in the same way that Jesus had gone out to the Jews.

Watch for the themes of salvation, forgiveness, empowerment through the Holy Spirit, and the radical reordering of priorities in society as you read in Luke for the balance of the church year. Every word of this gospel has intense meaning for our own struggle in the world today.

Our lectionary reading takes us from the prologue directly to the account of John the Baptist. (Chapters 1 and 2 of Luke are read, appropriately, at the end of Advent and during the Christmas season.) John's preaching confronts the established order. One cannot take his status with God for granted, he warns. "...every tree therefore that does not bear good fruit is cut down and thrown into the fire" (Luke 3:9b). These words must discomfit us if we examine our own understanding of what it means to be Christian and what we take for granted in our relationship with the Lord.

The emphasis on the poor and the setting free of the oppressed is shown early in Jesus' ministry in Galilee. Though Matthew and Mark report Jesus as going forth to preach after his baptism, only Luke records that he read Isaiah's words about bringing good news to the poor and setting the downtrodden free. This proclamation is followed immediately by Jesus' reminder to the people that God's word and power are not perceived by the people who consider themselves closest to the Lord. It was the people outside Israel who felt the healing power of God coming through the prophets Elijah and Elisha, Jesus pointed out.

Week of the Sunday closest to September 28

The Old Testament readings:

We'll be reading Hosea for the next nine days. Hosea lived in the northern kingdom of Israel shortly before it fell to the Assyrian conquerors in 721 B.C. As we read Saturday, Hosea married a prostitute, and, as he reflected on his troubled life with her, he began to see in his marriage a metaphor of God's relationship with Israel. God had called forth his bride, the Hebrew slaves in Egypt. He had made covenant with her in the wilderness, a covenant like that between a man and woman in marriage. But Israel, like Hosea's wife, Gomer, was unfaithful. She ran off to the gods of the Canaanites once the Hebrews entered the Promised Land. The Lord was Israel's king, but the people insisted on an earthly king and forced the prophet, Samuel, to anoint one. Thus, Israel became a nation like other nations. The people of Israel worshiped the Lord with no feelings or commitment.

As Gomer suffered for her unfaithfulness, so Israel must suffer. But that was not the last word for Gomer nor for Israel. God's steadfast love for his people rose above his anger and hurt. The Lord would call his people to restoration, into renewed relationship. He would take back the unfaithful bride, just as Hosea must take back his unfaithful wife. But the restoration would not come without suffering. Political powers to the north would be God's instrument to humble the unfaithful people. Then he would lead them back gently to the wilderness and restore the lost relationship.

We don't get the end of the story in the prophet's writing. He probably died before the fall of Israel to Assyria in 721 B.C., but he had seen this defeat coming and gave a theological understanding that went far beyond the immediate political implications.*

Interpreter's Dictionary of the Bible. Nashville & New York: Abingdon Press, 1962.

The Assyrians deported many of the most influential citizens of Israel to Assyria, replacing them with new settlers from the north. The territory that had been Israel became known as Samaria. The people in Jesus' time looked down on the Samaritans, feeling them to be still foreigners in a land set aside for God's chosen people. All that was left of David's once proud kingdom was the southern kingdom of Judah.

On Tuesday, Wednesday, and Thursday you will be reading the charges the Lord brought against his people. (Hosea used "Ephraim" as an alternative name for Israel. See Hosea 5:13.)

The specific acts of vengeance at the hands of the Assyrians are outlined by Hosea in the readings appointed for Friday and Saturday. Nothing less than the end of Israel as a nation state and of the kings of Israel as a line of rulers is in store for the unfaithful people.

The second readings:

Last week we read that Paul, like Jesus, was determined to return to Jerusalem. He must have known of the dangers to him there, but he felt he had no choice. He must return, and then he dreamed of going at last to the center of Roman power and pride, the city of Rome itself. After leaving Ephesus, he traveled through Greece to encourage the churches there and to continue the work of spreading the gospel. He then headed east toward Jerusalem. Notice on Monday the touching farewell scene with the elders from Ephesus. Ironically, it was Paul's Roman citizenship that saved him from his own people when he was arrested in Jerusalem. Remember, an overriding message in Acts reminds us again and again that nothing can stop the spread of the gospel. Now Paul will use Roman law as a vehicle to reach Rome. He will have the opportunity to appear before people of influence in the Roman hierarchy.

The Gospel readings:

Keep in mind the remarks I made last week about the Gospel of Luke as you read the assigned lessons this week. Friday you will begin reading Luke's counterpart to Matthew's Sermon on the Mount (Matt 5-7). This portion of Luke is sometimes referred to as the Sermon on the Plain since Luke states that Jesus talked to the people on level ground. This is a much shorter version of the "sermon." Actually, neither of these sections is a sermon in the true sense. The writers of Matthew and Luke collected some of Jesus' statements and placed those sayings together as one would string pearls to make a necklace. It was hard for the evangelists to know where and in what context Jesus made these statements. Placing the sayings together heightened their impact for the reader.

Week of the Sunday closest to October 5

The Old Testament reading:

We conclude our reading of Hosea Monday. The grim words of inevitable punishment to come are followed by the prophet's closing words that speak of restoration and God's abiding love. God is faithful to the covenant. He calls an unfaithful people back into covenant relationship, as Hosea had called Gomer back to live as his wife. This prophetic view of history helped some of the people of Israel and Judah find meaning in their struggle during those painful years.

Micah takes center stage Tuesday and for the following six days. The prophet was a poor country farmer who suffered at the hands of wealthy, powerful landlords. No wonder he felt called to speak out strongly against social and economic oppression. Moreover, the institution of Judaism was caught up in this oppression, he felt. The liturgy of the Temple was empty and without substance because it was not related to works of justice and integrity. Liturgy without justice was vile. It would appear that Micah was most active as a prophet just after the northern kingdom of Israel fell in 721 B.C. He could foresee similar destruction of the southern kingdom of Judah. Even the sacred city of David, Jerusalem, would not be spared. God would punish Judah, too, for injustice and unfaithfulness to the covenant. How do the words apply to us today, as a church, as a nation, as an economic entity?

As you get to the words of hope in chapter 4 Friday, note that the same words are found in Isaiah 2:2-4. A later editor was attempting to soften the harsh words of Micah with an appropriate insert of confidence in the Lord's mercy.

Saturday's reading reflects hope. Out of the district of Ephrathah will come a new ruler who will begin the restoration of Judah. The writer of the Gospel of Matthew saw this as a foretelling of Jesus (Matt 2:6). The last portion of Saturday's reading is the Lord's "disarmament treaty" with Judah. The Lord will tear away from Judah all articles of war and decadent religious practices so that the people will once more rely on him.

The second readings:
Our adventures in Acts continue through this week and next. Paul's appeal to Caesar saved him from being surrendered to the Jewish authorities, but his captivity dragged on as first one governor and then another was not quite sure how to handle his case. The governors' desire to keep favor with the Jews kept them from releasing Paul, and he languished in jail for over two years in Caesarea. However, Paul had limited freedom to talk with his followers and to encourage them, and imprisonment and court hearings provided him with opportunities to preach the gospel before important Roman authorities.

The Gospel readings:
This week we follow Jesus as he preaches, heals, and forgives the repentant sinners of Galilee. As you read the assigned chapters, note how values, priorities and accepted situations in life are reversed with the words and actions of Jesus. The sick become well and even the dead are raised. A woman considered an outcast becomes the one sent off in peace, in contrast to the self-righteous dinner host. In an age when women were considered inferior to men, we find Jesus being accompanied by women as well as men in his travels about Galilee. This would have been unheard of in Jesus' time. As the kingdom of God begins to be felt in the present age, the world is turned upside down. This, too, is good news, but it can be bad news for those who want to hold on to the old order and values. No wonder there was opposition to Jesus, to his followers, and to Paul. If the church today simply reflects the accepted standards, values, and positions of the rest of society, we are not living close enough to the gospel.

Week of the Sunday closest to October 12

The Old Testament readings:

We find ourselves in three different books of the Old Testament this week. Sunday's reading, inserted in Micah, was written by an unknown later prophet, probably from the period of King Manasseh (687-642 B.C.). Pagan cults were practiced in the Temple itself, and the people lived in an ever-deepening decadence. In this reading the Lord placed Judah on trial. Notice the closing words: "He has showed you, O man, what is good; and what does the Lord require of you but to do justice, and to love kindness, and to walk humbly with your God?" (Micah 6:8)

Tuesday through Thursday we read the delightful short story of Jonah, written sometime between 400-200 B.C. following the Babylonian Exile. *The Jerome Biblical Commentary* classifies Jonah as "didactic fiction," and so it appears to be. Read it with your sense of humor tuned in, for it is an amusing story. The self-righteous prophet, Jonah, wanted nothing more than the total destruction of the hated enemies of Judah, the people of Nineveh, but God called Jonah to save them from deserved destruction by calling them to repent and change their ways. Jonah resisted the assignment because he did not want to see them spared. This short story reveals the mercy of God that we, in our human frailty, have trouble identifying with at times. The Lord's mercy stands in sharp contrast to Jonah's petulance at seeing the city spared.

Friday we begin the reading of the Book of Ecclesiasticus. This writing is part of the Apocrypha and may not be in your Bible. (Since the Episcopal Church recognizes the books of the Apocrypha, I'd suggest you purchase a Bible that includes this important material.) Begin reading Ecclesiasticus and we'll talk about it next week.

The second readings:

We conclude our reading of the Acts of the Apostles this week. The adventure of Paul intensifies as he approaches Rome.

Paul had longed to go there; now he is brought as a prisoner. His situation serves only to increase his opportunities to heal and to preach the gospel. Nothing can stop the spread of the good news.

The book ends in mystery. We do not know what happened to Paul after his two years of virtual house arrest. Church tradition says he was martyred in Rome, but there is a hint from the closing verses of Acts that Paul may have been freed, at least for a time. Two years was the maximum time a Roman citizen could be held without trial. Chapter 28:30-31 describes the "whole of the two years" of his captivity with no reference to a trial or martyrdom. In any case, it is clear that Paul exercised his ministry in every possible way. Whatever happened, Paul was a living witness to the risen Christ through the power of the Holy Spirit.

The Gospel readings:
We continue to follow Jesus in his Galilean ministry this week. The stern conditions of following Jesus are made clear at several points in the assigned readings: "Take nothing for your journey. . .let him deny himself and take up his cross daily and follow me. . .for he who is least among you all is the one who is great."

Week of the Sunday closest to October 19

The Old Testament readings:

The title, Ecclesiasticus, is for "the church book." (This book may be listed in the Apocrypha in your Bible under the name of the author, Sirach.) The Greeks dominated the land of the Jews when Ecclesiasticus was written around 180 B.C. *The Jerome Biblical Commentary* tells us the book is "essentially an apology for Judaism. Writing to defend the religious and cultural heritage of Judaism against the challenge of Hellenism, Sirach sought to demonstrate to his fellow Jews in Palestine and the Diaspora, and also to well-meaning pagans, that true wisdom resides in Israel. He accomplishes his purpose by producing a synthesis of revealed religion and empirical wisdom" (page 541). (Diaspora is a term meaning the dispersed Jews living outside Palestine.)

A few weeks ago as we studied the Book of Job, I mentioned that wisdom literature differs from the majority of the biblical writings in that it stands apart from the social and historical context of the faith and looks at how the individual finds meaning and purpose in his or her life. The many "how to" books in airport gift shops are an example of some contemporary "wisdom" literature but, at a more profound level, we find contemporary wisdom literature in poetry, drama, and in the visual arts. This is the kind of literature and art that helps us look at the deepest questions of our lives and find meaning in the process.

An ingredient of Jewish wisdom literature missing in the contemporary counterparts I've given, however, is the understanding that the origins of all true wisdom is God. The beginning of wisdom is awe (fear) of God. (Fear, in the Bible, does not mean being afraid of God, but rather standing in awe or reverence of God.) To seek God is to seek ultimate truth. Moreover, this wisdom that is God has existed through all creation. That's what we read in Ecclesiasticus last week: "Wisdom was created before all things, and prudent understanding from eternity" (Ecclus 1:4).

Notice in the reading for last Friday that wisdom is personified: "The Lord himself created wisdom; he saw her and apportioned her, he poured her out upon all his works. She dwells with all flesh according to his gift, and he supplied her to those who love him" (Ecclus 1:9-10). Wisdom is usually referred to in the feminine gender, rather than the masculine.

With the personification of wisdom in mind, read the prologue to the Gospel of John (John 1:1-18): "In the beginning was the Word, and the Word was with God, and the Word was God..." The Word is the Wisdom of God. In the New Testament we discover that the Wisdom or Word of God became flesh (incarnate) in Jesus. This Wisdom touched us personally and physically in the figure of a man and continues to touch us personally today through the Holy Spirit dwelling in us.

Now begin reading Ecclesiasticus and notice the calls for justice and fair treatment of the poor. Though the words are addressed to the individual, they still are political and social statements that reflect the high calling of the covenant people.

The second readings:
This week we begin a three and a half weeks' study of the Book of Revelation. Because so much confusion and mystery surrounds this book, people tend to shy away from it, or they take it as literal prophecy of what is to come. Before you start to read it, therefore, you need to keep a few things in mind. The Book of Revelation is a distinctive type of literature called "apocalypticism," from the Greek word meaning to reveal or to uncover, as in uncovering a mystery. This unique style of literature, *The Interpreter's Bible Dictionary* tells us, originated in the Persian religious cults and gradually was taken into Jewish literary tradition during and after the Babylonian Exile. Look over the Old Testament books of Daniel and Ezekiel and compare them with the material you are reading in Revelation these weeks for the source of some of the imagery in Revelation.

A few of the characteristics of apocalyptic literature are a use of symbols, numbers, and strange visions mediated by angels and heavenly beings, and a dualistic struggle between the forces of good and evil. The good news is that the force of good wins out in the final struggle with the forces of evil, and all who follow the force of evil are utterly banished and destroyed forever.

Apocalypticism rises out of an oppressed people who see their hopes dashed in the continuing oppression of foreign powers. These powers take on the characteristics of evil. The hope that gives courage to the people is that the power of God will finally defeat the power of evil and restore the faithful to a new kingdom prepared for them. Unlike early biblical literature that concentrates God's activity within the normal realms of history and revelation, apocalyptic literature shows God as acting outside of history in strange visions of triumphant power. The final message is that the enemy will be defeated and the good people who remained faithful to God will be triumphant.

The coded nature of this style of literature hides the true meaning from the oppressor while giving hope to the oppressed. In this sense, I would term this as "underground" literature. The Book of Revelation was written at just such a time of oppression. A majority of scholars place the date of writing at about 95 A.D., during the reign of the Roman emperor, Domitian, an emperor who ruthlessly persecuted the Christian churches of the empire.

Now begin your reading of the book. Place yourself in the historic period of the book's origin. Identify with oppressed Christians living in the world today. What does the book say to them and to us as we struggle in a world that seems to be breaking apart under principalities and powers of the present age?

We begin our reading in Revelation with a vivid picture of the rewarding of the righteous placed in stark juxtaposition to the trials of the wicked. The 144,000 is a symbolic number representing all those who have been purified through persecution and martyrdom as Christians.

Revelation gives us some beautiful glimpses of early Christian worship. The writer embellishes the worship practices of the New Testament church by envisioning what that worship will be like when God's reign is fulfilled. For example, in Revelation 7:10-12 we see some fragments of liturgical texts used by the early Christians in their worship: "Salvation belongs to our God who sits upon the throne, and to the Lamb!...Amen! Blessings and glory and wisdom and thanksgiving and honor and power and might be to our God for ever and ever! Amen."

In contrast to the vision of victorious joy of the 144,000 who were redeemed, we turn next to the terrible plagues that fall upon those who represent the principalities and powers of the present order in the world. Have the plagues of Exodus in mind as you read from Revelation this week.

The Gospel readings:
The feeling of the Gospel of Luke changes this week as we move into another major section of the work. Jesus "...set his face to go to Jerusalem" and prepared himself and his disciples for what he knew would happen there as he came face to face with the opposition of the established authorities. Read the assigned passages with a sense of dread of what is to come. When Jesus spoke of the hardships of being an apostle, he felt the shadow of the cross even as he talked.

Week of the Sunday closest to October 26

The Old Testament readings:

You may be getting bogged down these days with our friend, Sirach. Though some of his shared wisdom is lofty sayings pointing to the just demands of God, many passages are rather mundane: "Do not become a beggar by feasting with borrowed money, when you have nothing in your purse" (18:33). This sounds like Visa and Mastercharge were already well established some 180 years before Jesus! But there are beautiful passages in this book. Enjoy Tuesday's poem to wisdom and note again the feminine gender and personification of Wisdom. There are portions of the Gospel of John that we read several weeks ago that do not sound unlike our present reading in Ecclesiasticus.

The second readings:

And our second readings this week may be heavy going at times, too, but look behind the symbolism for a suffering, persecuted people looking for signs of hope for God's kingdom that is coming. There is no need to try to pin down the meaning of the rather bizarre symbols in the book. Many people have turned to Revelation to forecast the end of the world and the second coming of Christ, but remember the nature of the literature we are reading. At the same time appreciate the mystery of the writing. Part of the important message of apocalypticism for all of us is that God's powers are not limited to what we can understand and control. The Lord works in history, and the Lord works in awesome mysteries of creation and new creation. Think of the poetry of the Book of Job. We were not there when the foundations of creation were laid, nor can we fathom the mind of God. It is in symbol, poetry, and vision that we reach for the truth that always lies beyond us. The overall message of Revelation is as relevant for us today as it was for the persecuted Christians of the first century. God, not man and woman, is in control of creation ultimately. We can say this even as we face the possibility of nuclear holocaust. For those who would destroy creation in nuclear war, this message must be heard as God's judgment. For those who live under the shadow of that destructive power, Revelation provides a hopeful statement that God's creation cannot ultimately be destroyed.

Monday's reading opens with a description of two witnesses (symbolized at first as two lampstands and two olive trees) who stand before the evil powers of the world to witness for God. In the end, nothing can destroy these faithful witnesses. On Tuesday we turn from promised woe for the enemies of Christ to promised victory for the faithful. Notice another possible fragment from an early Christian liturgical text (Rev 11:17-18). The joyful hymn of praise for God's ultimate victory is followed by a description of a vision of the struggle between a woman and her child and a vicious dragon. Here we see a picture of the terrible struggle between the powers of the world and the church; the church will not in the end be devoured any more than the woman was devoured.

The "beast rising out of the sea" is introduced to us on Friday. In coded language, the writer describes the Roman Empire's ruthless persecution of the church. The closing words assigned for this week's reading refer to the strange number 666, probably a numerical scheme in which numbers represent letters of the alphabet. The designation would seem to refer to the Roman emperor Nero who died before Revelation was written.

The Gospel readings:

We continue our walk with Jesus this week as he moves deliberately toward his appointment with crucifixion. Along the road he encounters those who would tempt him away from the fulfillment of his saving role in history. The Pharisees and Saducees could not accept his radical interpretation of the covenant. His own disciples and those who drew close to hear his word along the road were not much more receptive. Those who would follow Jesus must know the cost of their discipleship. The time is short.

Decision is the demand of Jesus in Monday's reading. When

one is cleansed of "unclean spirits" one must replace allegiance to evil with allegiance to Christ. A passive neutrality will not do. The same point is made to the woman who cries out to Jesus about the blessedness of his mother in giving him birth. "Blessed rather are those who hear the word of God and keep it!" is Jesus' sharp response, read on Tuesday.

Jesus has been healing and teaching among the people since his baptism by John. His words and actions have been a clear indication that the promised judgment and deliverance of God is close, and yet the people stand around asking for signs of God's presence among them! How could any sign be clearer than what Jesus has been doing among the people, he asks in Monday's reading? The people of Nineveh were quick to repent when the prophet Jonah preached to them. The Queen of Sheba visited King Solomon (1 Kings 10:1-13) to listen to his wisdom. The people of Nineveh and the Queen of Sheba, enemies and aliens of Israel, will stand in judgment over Israel in the days to come, for they at least had sense enough to respond to the preaching and wisdom of God.

Wednesday's reading is a strong condemnation of the Pharisees and lawyers who challenge Jesus' words and acts. To appreciate his denunciation of the religious hierarchy of his day, replace the words "Pharisees and lawyers" with "church leaders."

Jesus' words read on Thursday are a grim foretaste of the Christian persecutions to come. Read these words with thoughts of Christian persecutions that continue where the gospel confronts oppressive leaders. Bishop Desmond Tutu and many other Christians in South Africa find themselves facing imprisonment and even death as they witness to the justice that Christ demands. The gospel is a radical power that threatens the unjust orders that enslave people in political and economic servitude.

A difficult statement greets us Thursday: "And every one who speaks a word against the Son of man will be forgiven; but he who blasphemes against the Holy Spirit will not be forgiven. And when they bring you before the synagogues and the rulers and the authorities, do not be anxious how or what you are to answer or what you are to say; for the Holy Spirit will teach you in that very hour what you are to say" (Luke 12:10-12). The Interpreter's Bible explains that "...blasphemy against the Holy Spirit is probably to be understood in the light of verse 12. The unbeliever who speaks against Christ will be forgiven but not the believer who refuses to confess faith when supernaturally prompted to do so." (*The Interpreter's Bible,* volume 8, page 224, Abingdon Press)

On Friday, the emphasis shifts from confrontation and warnings of judgment to instruction on discipleship. The values of the disciple are not to be the values of society, Jesus warns.

Week of the Sunday closest to November 2

The Old Testament readings:

Words of vengeance greet us as we begin our week in Ecclesiasticus. The writer prays for a restoration based on the utter destruction of the enemy. Christians tend to shy away from some of the more vindictive psalms, feeling them unfit for public reading in the church, yet there is vengeance, also, in the words of Revelation we are reading. The descriptions of the final battle in which the forces of evil are crushed forever declares in vivid terms the annihilation of the enemy. When a people feels the crushing oppression of power, the response is anger, whether that power be the Greeks of Sirach's time, the Romans of the first century, or the martial law of totalitarian regimes in our day.

The reading for Tuesday is included in the eucharistic lectionary for Labor Day. Ecclesiasticus touches each aspect of life as the writer reflects on the meaning of human existence under God. Wednesday's reading reminds us of the response of God to Job, read several weeks ago. As our biblical ancestors came into the land of Canaan after the Exodus, they understood God as the Lord of history. Their Canaanite neighbors, on the other hand, worshiped the gods of nature and natural forces. Gradually our Hebrew ancestors-in-faith realized that the one God of Israel was Lord of both history and creation. Thus, we find both canticles of appreciation for God's acts in history as well as songs of praise for his acts in creation.

The second readings:

In reading the Book of Revelation, remember that one of the characteristics of apocalyptic literature was the writing about the present moment as though it were a historical event. Thus, read "Babylon" as "Rome" and the beasts who will fall to destruction as the Roman emperors and the powers of Rome. Remember the "underground" nature of this literature. A persecuted people can more safely denounce an empire that has already fallen a generation or more ago than it can the present one. Revelation is truly inflammatory literature, written to give people hope in the face of hideous persecution. The content of such a message must be carefully couched in references to the past and symbols that speak of strange beasts and mystic numbers in case the wrong people read the tract. Feel the sense of tragic history happening as you read this important last book of the Bible. Think of the kinds of underground literature that is produced today by peoples who live under oppression. God's will be done!

Another liturgical text is embedded in the closing words assigned for Monday: "Blessed are the dead who die in the Lord henceforth...that they may rest from their labors, for their deeds follow them." Canticle 19 from Morning Prayer, "The Song of the Redeemed," is another liturgical text found in this week's reading from Revelation. The church still offers these beautiful words to God in worship today. We sing in harmony with those who struggled and died under the persecutions of the early church.

Notice the pattern of Revelation. We move from scenes of judgment for the wicked to scenes of joy for the redeemed. These scenes grow increasingly sharp as we progress through the book.

The fall of Rome and the destruction of Nero's power is depicted in the readings at the end of the week. For "Babylon" read "Rome." This is underground literature, remember. Someone from outside the Christian circle would not see that the judgment and hatred was leveled against the present empire. The image grows of the beautiful city of God standing in contrast with the crumbling city that represents the Roman Empire. The merchants and traders of this present age lament the loss of the city's power.

The Gospel readings:
The necessity for the disciple to make a radical decision for Christ is again emphasized as we begin our week in Luke. Jesus came to force a decision on the believer. There can be no compromise with the proclamation of the gospel. Acceptance

of one's discipleship will inevitably bring conflict even within families. Time was running out. Jesus foresaw his "baptism" of suffering and death that would inaugurate the reign of God. Disciples will find themselves facing the same baptism as Jesus.

The demand for decision continues to be the theme as the week progressses. Jesus is questioned about the death of people killed as a result of persecution and accident. Was their death a punishment from God? No, he assures them, but let their deaths be a warning of your own need to act now. Life can be snuffed out in an instant. God expects the disciple to bear fruit. Jesus' warnings about decisive action for the gospel is heightened with the parable of the fig tree: "And if it bears fruit next year, well and good, but if not, you can cut it down" (Luke 13:9).

The words we read this week must be taken very seriously. Our quest for power and success in the world must not come before our primary task of standing with Christ for justice and healing. That is what it means to bear fruit in the kingdom of God. Pious language or complacent participation in church life cannot be equated with following Christ.

On Saturday we find ourselves sitting at table with Jesus in the home of a Pharisee. The dinner table conversation provides a metaphor that Jesus used to talk about Christian humility.

Week of the Sunday closest to November 9

The Old Testament readings:

We're approaching the end of the liturgical year now. Advent is near, a season of penance and preparation for the coming of the Lord at the end of the age and a time for reflecting on the coming of the Lord as Jesus. His coming means a time of judgment. We must examine ourselves as Christians. Are we living within the covenant that we accepted at baptism? We must examine our nation, our businesses, our homes, and our society. How does our life reflect the life the Lord holds out for us, the abundant life of the gospel? What must the church say to a world that often denies the abundant life to the many so that a more abundant life can be grasped by the few? This is the mood of the church as we move toward Advent and the beginning of a new year for the church. The lectionary readings reflect that mood.

Sunday we finish with Ecclesiasticus and begin Monday reading the prophet, Joel. To appreciate Joel, imagine the time when the Jews had returned from Babylonian exile to their own land of Judah. During the exile our biblical ancestors had longed for this restoration, but once back in their own land, they found life far more harsh and bitter than they had anticipated. The second Temple was built on the ruins of the first, but it lacked the beauty and wonder of their memories of past glory. Being home did not automatically bring restoration, the people found. Decadence in national life and in religious practices soon crept in. The joy and laughter of homecoming was replaced by a cynicism and live-for-the-day attitude.

Then came a plague of locusts which ate through the land like an invading army. Joel suffered this plague with the rest of the people, but he saw in it a sign that God was calling the people to repentance. They were to prepare themselves for the day of the Lord, when the Lord would come to judge all peoples. When the plague ceased, Joel saw it as a sign of forgiveness. The judgment would come, Joel announced, but it would be against those who plagued Judah.

Your reading in the Old Testament will be simpler this week. Joel's description of the plague is vivid. We are drawn easily into the situation. The two verses from Joel 2, assigned for Tuesday, along with the entire text for Wednesday, are in the eucharistic lectionary for Ash Wednesday. Lent, for us, is an annual plague in the sense that it sends us out in penance and contrition to prepare for the Lord's coming and judgment.

Friday's reading may also be familiar to you because it is assigned as an option for the feast of Pentecost. The day is coming when God's Spirit will be poured out on all peoples. Beginning with chapter 3, Joel turns to a harsh judgment that will come to Judah's enemies. Notice in Saturday's reading that the call for peace so eloquently phrased by Isaiah—". . .they shall beat their swords into plowshares, and their spears into pruning hooks. . ." (2:4)—is reversed in Joel's writing: "Beat your plowshares into swords, and your pruning hooks into spears. . ." (3:10). The nations must be punished for their actions against God's people.

The second readings:

We finish our reading of Revelation Wednesday with chapter 19. The last two chapters are left for another time, but I'd suggest that you take a little time this week to read them. Some of the most beautiful and hopeful words in scripture are found there.

The evil city of Rome is destroyed. From the lament for the loss of Rome given by those who traded with the empire comes a contrasting scene of praise and thanksgiving sung by the victorious Christians as they gather in God's presence in heaven. The second hymn sung from heaven (Rev 19:6-8) uses the metaphor of the marriage between the Lamb (Christ) and the Bride (the faithful church). This imagery, borrowed from the Old Testament, is reflected in the marriage liturgy of The Book of Common Prayer: "It (marriage) signifies to us the mystery of the union between Christ and his Church. . ." (BCP, p. 423). "O God, you have so consecrated the covenant of marriage that in it is represented the spiritual unity between Christ and his

Church..." (BCP, p. 431). Marriage between man and woman becomes a metaphor of our relationship with God. That is the note on which we leave Revelation.

Taken as a whole, Revelation is an important book that crowns and completes the biblical story. We may not be suffering the persecutions of the early Christians or of contemporary Christians who live under oppression, but each one of us needs to remember daily that God is ultimately triumphant in creation. We are chosen as God's people, empowered with God's Spirit, and given a vision of life that surpasses human understanding. This is the word that sends us forth in the face of seemingly insurmountable difficulties ready to proclaim the new day that brings the abundant life in Christ.

On Thursday we begin reading the epistle of James. Scholars disagree over whether this letter was actually written by James, the brother of Jesus, or by a writer who lived later in the first century, or even early in the second century. The later dating seems more natural to me as I relate to the writing. James writes for the church, giving guidelines for Christian living. He has a strong sense of social justice for the poor. We are to be doers of the word, and not just hearers. Friday's reading is a confrontation to those who "listen and do not obey." Look at the definition of true religion in the closing verse of chapter l.

The Gospel readings:
The Cost of Discipleship, the title of a book by the Christian martyr, Dietrich Bonhoeffer, could well be the title for Monday's and Tuesday's readings. The parable of the wedding feast is a confrontation to the institutional church of our day. We are invited to do the Lord's work, but, like the Jews of Jesus' time, it is often the outcasts whom the Lord must bring in to sit at table with him. We are bound by our possessions and worldly responsibilities, too busy and involved to respond. Renounce that life that holds us back, is the word we hear today.

Chapter 15 provides us with three parables of God's mercy. The parable of the prodigal son, I feel, is the most beautiful statement of God's love and mercy in the Bible. The lost son is not accepted because he deserves forgiveness. He is not even particularly remorseful when he gets up from the pigsty. He's hungry! Yet the father is "moved with pity." This parable calls us back to God on those many days when we think we've blown it, or that God has forgotten us in our pigsty.

Week of the Sunday closest to November 16

The Old Testament readings:

This week we look at two prophets, beginning with Habakkuk and ending with Malachi. The next time a member of Jehovah's Witnesses comes knocking on your door with a copy of their paper, *The Watchtower,* in hand you can greet them with Habakkuk 2:1, the origin of that paper's title: "I will take my stand to watch, and station myself on the tower, and look forth to see what he (the Lord) will say to me. . . ." This brief greeting will serve as some proof to your caller that scripture is no stranger to you!

Habakkuk probably wrote right before the Babylonians swept into Judah and deported many of the Jews to Babylon. He raised angry questions to God; how can the Lord, who demands justice and compassion of the people, use such an unjust and cruel people to punish the Jews? What kind of justice is that? How can the Lord remain silent ". . .when the wicked swallows up the man more righteous than he?" Perhaps, just perhaps, you may have dared to raise such a question yourself at least once or twice in your life. It's always heartening to know you have friends in high places, isn't it? Habakkuk has walked your road before you. The hinge point of this brief book is the first four verses of the second chapter. Mounting the watchtower to better perceive the word and actions of the Lord, Habakkuk perceives that ". . .the righteous shall live by his faith." From that point on the prophet speaks of the coming of inevitable punishment for those who do evil in the sight of the Lord.

Malachi is a brief book written at about the same time as the Book of Joel. The writer—the title of the book means "messenger" and is not the name of the prophet—was deeply disturbed at the sloppy keeping of the Mosaic Law by the returned exiles. He decried the decadent practices of Temple worship by both priests and people. The prophet called the people back to a true covenant worship and response to God. The writer looked forward to the day when the people would at last respond to the messengers of the Lord, whose words would cut through to the people like a refiner's fire shapes precious metal. (Jesus referred to this passage when he talked about the role John the Baptist played as a messenger of God.) Once the people turned back to the Lord they would see the difference, the writer felt. The upright person would prosper, and the evil would fall of their own weight. When the people began to tithe again, the Lord would ". . .open the windows of heaven. . ." once again (Mal 3:10).

The second readings:

The Epistle of James continues to be our focus this week. Social justice and compassion for the poor and the oppressed are the marks of a faithful person, James pointed out: "So faith by itself, if it has no works, is dead" (2:17). Then he goes on to outline what an active faith looks like in the Christian community. Faith shapes values and relationships and responses to the needs of others in the community. Faith calls the wealthy to task for relying on themselves and oppressing their workers in order to gain more. Friday's reading includes the call to lay hands on the sick and to confess sins to one another. Prayer and confession lead to healing and wholeness in the body of Christ. The practice of public confession or confession to priest or lay person has its roots in this simple message of healing.

The Gospel readings:

Jesus approaches Jerusalem and the cross, preparing his disciples for the days to come. This week we read parables and teachings meant to guide the life of the disciples. Compassion and service to the poor, prayer and faith, and eyes open for the signs of the coming kingdom are essentials of the Christian life.

Week of the Sunday closest to November 23

The Old Testament readings:

Our last Old Testament book of the church year is a later one, dated about 200 B.C. Keep my remarks about apocalyptic literature in mind as you read Zechariah. We start at chapter nine because the book is really two separate writings by two authors done at different times in Judah's history. Our present author lived during the period when the Greeks controlled the land of the Jews. The great day of the Lord is coming when Israel will be cleansed of sinful practices once and for all, the prophet wrote. Israel's enemies will be finally destroyed. Beyond the destruction will be a time of universal peace, when the whole world will stream to Jerusalem to worship the one and true god. The writings end with a picture of perfect peace and rejoicing in Jerusalem.

Watch for familiar phrases in your reading this week. The gospel writers quoted from Zechariah in several places to illuminate their words about Jesus as Savior. Zechariah 9:9-10 are the familiar words heard on Palm Sunday. The Messiah comes riding on a beast of peace, the donkey, rather than a beast of war, the horse. Zechariah 12:10 talks about the nations looking with compassion on the one they have pierced. You'll find reference to that in John 19:37 in connection with Jesus' crucifixion. The book closes with a reference to the time when ". . .there shall no longer be a trader in the house of the Lord." The elimination of traders who often took advantage of the pilgrim worshipers in the Temple is one of Zechariah's signs of the new age of the Messiah. Jesus' driving the money-changers from the Temple was a symbolic carrying out of this prophecy.

The second readings:

Our second readings this week are a potpourri of selections from the epistles that help us reflect on the meaning and purpose of our lives as Christians living in community as the body of Christ. God's plan of salvation is outlined by St. Paul, and our call to build and be that body is proclaimed. This makes a fitting end to our year of living as Christ's people in the church. It is a time of reflecting on our lives before we move ahead into the new year of the church with the First Sunday of Advent next week.

The Gospel readings:
Jesus' concern for the poor, the weak, and the outcast is expressed in much of the reading this week. The children are blessed. Zaccheus is honored. Becoming poor for the sake of the kingdom is held up as an ideal. The parable of the talents is sometimes used to justify capitalism and to bless industrious folk who invest their money well, but note the context of this parable. It has nothing to do with investing money and everything to do with using the time between Jesus' departure and his coming again productively *for the kingdom*.

The parable comes right before Jesus' entry into Jerusalem. This is the last story Jesus tells in Luke's narrative before he arrives at the gates of the city. In a sense, the parable serves as a summary of all the teaching about life after the resurrection we've been reading about these past few weeks. "I'm leaving you in charge," Jesus might have said. "Don't blow it." Produce the appropriate fruit of the kingdom, was the message and warning to his disciples then and now.

Next week we begin at the beginning. The First Sunday of Advent marks the beginning of a new year in the liturgical calendar. Turn to the opening of the daily office lectionary, page 936 of The Book of Common Prayer. Start your reading with week of 1 Advent, year one. Follow the readings on the left pages all the way through the church year. Happy New Year!